THE MEISSEN MANUFACTORY: ART, INDUSTRY, AND IDENTITY ACROSS THREE CENTURIES

Dr Frederik Coene

ISBN: 979-8-90417-718-8 (Kindle Edition)
ISBN: 979-8-90417-718-5 (Paperback Edition)

CONTENTS

INTRODUCTION

For centuries, the secret of porcelain production represented one of the most coveted forms of knowledge in Europe, and porcelain imported from China occupied a unique position in European culture. Known as '*white gold*,' it represented artistic refinement and technological achievement, and its manufacture in Europe became an ambitious goal for many monarchs.

The establishment of the porcelain manufactory in Meissen in the early eighteenth century marked a decisive turning point. As the first European producer of hard-paste porcelain, Meissen succeeded where others had failed, establishing a tradition that continues into the present. More than three hundred years later, it remains one of the few manufactories still committed to preserving elements of its traditional craftsmanship.

Yet behind this achievement lay a far more complex and human story. The history of Meissen is not simply one of innovation and success. As Ulrich Pietsch and Peter Ufer have written, it is also a history of '*people with crazy ideas, unwavering belief, a technical mind, amazing passion, infinite diligence,*' alongside '*remarkable visionaries, creative artists, faithful patrons, notable professionals,*' and equally of '*mistakes, forgeries, suffering and defeats.*'[1]

Although hundreds of books and articles have examined specific moments in Meissen's history, relatively few offer a broad and accessible overview. This monograph provides a structured synthesis of the existing literature and research, exploring the artistic qualities of Meissen porcelain and the political and economic circumstances that have shaped the manufactory. These factors have often influenced its creative direction. As the manufactory was owned first by the Saxon royal house and later by the Saxon state, political influence has played a particularly important role—more so than with many competitors.

The chapters are organised according to major artistic periods and trends, though this division should not be regarded as rigid, as stylistic development at Meissen was largely continuous. The present study focuses on the creation of new objects, which does not necessarily correspond to patterns of demand; for instance, in the early twentieth century, Jugendstil was critically acclaimed but represented only a small proportion of sales. The periodisation adopted here may therefore differ from that used in other studies, some of which rely on alternative chronologies or on changes in the Crossed Swords mark.

Some periods are explored in greater detail than others, reflecting the importance of certain eras and individuals in shaping Meissen's artistic richness and reputation. The Höroldt–Kändler period, for example, was one of the most creative and productive. The works produced during that time influenced both taste and production for many generations, thus warranting particular attention. However, even less successful eras have played a role in shaping the manufactory's long and complex history—one of which it can justifiably be proud.

A recurring theme throughout this book is the dual nature of the Meissen manufactory. On the one hand, it is a commercial enterprise that must generate profit; on the other, it has long seen itself as a leader in the artistic development of porcelain. This dual role has often created tension for its leadership, as the balance between artistic ambition and financial reality is not always easily maintained. The financial challenges of recent years can be seen as part of this ongoing struggle and should be understood within a broader historical context. Difficult periods are nothing new for the manufactory; without them, its history, and perhaps even its identity, would be fundamentally different.

ORIGINS OF PORCELAIN AND FIRST EUROPEAN ATTEMPTS

The exact moment of porcelain's invention cannot be determined, as it appears to have developed gradually from earlier Chinese ceramics. The composition of certain ceramic objects dating from before 1000 BC already bears compositional similarities to that of porcelain, although these pieces were fired at lower temperatures and cannot yet be considered true porcelain. However, by the time of the Eastern Han dynasty (25–220 AD), a greenish, high-fired ceramic often described as proto-porcelain or early celadon was being produced in Zhejiang province.

Driven in part by the growing popularity of tea drinking, which required suitable vessels, and by increasing exports to the Islamic world, the production of celadon in Zhejiang and white Xing ware from Hebei province expanded significantly during the Tang dynasty (618–907). This development continued during the Song dynasty (960–1279). In 1004, Emperor Zhenzong officially designated the region of Jingdezhen in Jiangxi province as the centre of imperial porcelain production—a status it would retain for nearly nine centuries.

Jingdezhen, rich in deposits of high-quality kaolin—one of the essential components of porcelain paste—became particularly renowned during the Ming dynasty (1368–1644) for its porcelain decorated with cobalt blue. At the same time, 'blanc de Chine' from the Dehua kilns in Fujian province gained widespread popularity. It was also during this period that Chinese porcelain began to be exported to Europe in significant quantities, where it was often referred to as '*white gold*' due to the high prices it commanded. Although Chinese porcelain remained highly sought after during the Qing dynasty (1644–1912), it increasingly faced competition from European production.

Porcelain production was not exclusive to China. In Korea, celadon and white porcelain flourished during the Goryeo period (918–1392), with production continuing in subsequent centuries until disrupted by Japanese invasions in the late sixteenth century. In Japan, porcelain production began in the early seventeenth century in the Arita region. This porcelain became widely known in Europe as Imari porcelain, named after the port from which it was exported. The Kakiemon style of decoration was particularly popular and was later imitated by European manufactories, including Meissen, Chelsea, Worcester, Vienna, and Chantilly, although not always through direct copies of Japanese originals.

Given the high demand for and prestige associated with porcelain, European craftsmen were keen to discover its method of production. However, the technical knowledge remained closely guarded in East Asia. While Europe possessed extensive experience in earthenware and ceramics, it took several centuries for artisans to understand and reproduce the complex process required to create porcelain—combining characteristics of both ceramics and glass.

Despite these developments in East Asia, Europe remained technologically far behind. The earliest recorded European experiments date back to the fifteenth century in Venice. Around 1470, the alchemist Maestro Antuonio is said to have produced vessels from a light and translucent material. As none of these objects have survived, the nature of his achievement remains unclear. In 1518, Leonardo Peutinger, also working in Venice, reportedly created a form of '*transparent porcelain*,' though again, no surviving examples allow for further assessment.

The first truly successful imitation of Chinese porcelain in Europe was produced around 1575 in Florence and is known as Medici porcelain, named after its patron. Influenced in part by Middle Eastern ceramic techniques, it nevertheless proved too costly to sustain, and the manufactory ceased production after roughly a decade. Further notable attempts were made in the 1670s by the French potter Louis Poterat in Rouen and the English potter and alchemist John Dwight in Fulham, London. However, neither succeeded in producing porcelain on a commercially viable scale.

These early European experiments resulted in what is now known as soft-paste porcelain, which differs significantly from true hard-paste porcelain. Soft-paste porcelain has a different composition, is less durable, and is fired at lower temperatures; its glaze is also more susceptible to scratching. One of the first commercially significant production of soft-paste porcelain began in 1702 with the establishment of the Saint-Cloud factory, following the 'rediscovery' of the technique by its owner, Pierre Chicaneau.

Despite these advances, European porcelain remained, in essence, an imitation—technically ingenious, but fundamentally distinct from its Asian counterpart. The ambition to uncover the secret of true porcelain persisted across Europe, driven not only by scientific curiosity but also by the economic and political interests of the courts that sponsored such experiments.

It was within this environment—where alchemy, science, and courtly ambition often intersected—that the decisive breakthrough occurred. In the early eighteenth century, a series of experiments conducted under royal patronage in the Electorate of Saxony led to the successful production of hard-paste porcelain in 1708. This achievement marked a decisive turning point in the European quest for 'true' porcelain and the beginning of a new chapter in the history of European craftsmanship.

THE INVENTION OF EUROPEAN HARD-PASTE PORCELAIN

Although most authors credit Johann Friedrich Böttger (1682-1719) with the invention of European hard-paste porcelain, it is more accurate to view it as a collective achievement. Ehrenfried Walther von Tschirnhaus (1651-1708) laid important groundwork that formed the basis for Böttger's trials, and may have been close to achieving the breakthrough himself. Gottfried Pabst von Ohain (1656-1729) provided various mineral samples, including the '*white clay*' (kaolin) from Aue. Dr. Jacob Bartholomäi focused on paste preparation, working to find the optimum mix of ingredients. A dedicated team of assistants surrounded Böttger, undeterred by the hazards posed by toxic fumes. Finally, without the financial support of Augustus II the Strong (1670–1733), Elector of Saxony and King of Poland, the development of European porcelain would likely have been delayed or taken a different course. In the early eighteenth century, Saxony's lucrative mining industry made it one of the more economically prosperous regions of Europe, providing Augustus the Strong with ample resources to finance research into porcelain production.

It is important to emphasize that European hard-paste porcelain is best understood as a process of invention rather than a simple rediscovery. While the composition of the porcelain paste and the related firing process may be similar to those of Asian porcelain, the technical differences are significant, with major implications for the application of glaze and paint. East Asian porcelain typically relied on different raw material compositions, often involving feldspathic rocks such as petuntse, resulting in different firing properties and decorative possibilities, particularly in relation to overglaze enamel decoration. Finally, Asian porcelain has a different glaze, often characterised by a more translucent glaze, which in some cases appears greenish or bluish.

Interestingly, the invention of European porcelain is linked to alchemy, an ancient branch of chemistry and philosophy that aimed, among other things, at the transmutation of metals. In the early 18th century, many royal leaders supported experiments in this field, believing that success in turning ordinary metals into gold would provide unrestricted wealth, as well as political power and domination.

In 1696, Johann Friedrich Böttger, whose stepfather had introduced him to geometry, pyrotechnics, engineering, and other scientific disciplines, began an apprenticeship at Friedrich Zorn's pharmacy in Berlin. However, the 14-year-old's ambitions extended beyond pharmaceutical knowledge. He developed a keen interest in alchemy and began experimenting in the pharmacy's laboratory, much to his employer's displeasure. In 1701, Böttger attempted to assuage Zorn's scepticism by staging a demonstration. The young alchemist deceived his mentor and other witnesses into believing they had seen him transmute 18 silver coins into gold. Despite Böttger's request for secrecy, the rumour quickly spread, eventually reaching Prussian King Frederick I. Desperate for funds to support his lavish lifestyle and driven by ambitions to expand his power and prestige, the king summoned the young man, hoping he could fulfil these aspirations.

Realizing the danger if his deception were exposed, Böttger fled to Wittenberg in neighbouring Saxony. There, Saxon authorities arrested him. Elector Augustus the Strong of Saxony, intrigued by the fugitive alchemist, requested custody and had him transferred to Dresden, where he was placed under protective custody. Claiming to possess the ability to transmute silver into gold, he remained in the royal castle, provided with a laboratory and assistants to continue his experiments. Augustus the Strong appointed Gottfried Pabst von Ohain, a respected scientist and manager of the royal silver mines, to supervise Böttger's work. A few months later, the alchemist escaped but was soon apprehended in Austria. Following his repeated promises to produce vast quantities of gold and von Ohain's pleas for leniency, Augustus the Strong spared his life.

In 1702, Johann Friedrich Böttger first met Ehrenfried Walther von Tschirnhaus, who was studying mines throughout Saxony and had focused his research and experiments on porcelain production. This multi-disciplinary scientist—who maintained connections with Gottfried Wilhelm Leibniz, Barukh Spinoza, and Isaac Newton—travelled to Delft in Holland, and Saint-Cloud in France, to study the production of faience and frit porcelain. He made important discoveries, such as that some minerals, though unmeltable alone, become fusible when mixed with others. However, his experiments leaned rather toward glass production.[2] Böttger and von Tschirnhaus met regularly to exchange views on their experiments, and in 1704, von Tschirnhaus was appointed to supervise the young alchemist, who had still not fulfilled his promise to provide Augustus the Strong with tons of gold. Although Böttger was uninterested in porcelain production, he researched ceramics to create durable crucibles for his experiments. In September 1705, Böttger was moved from Dresden to the Albrechtsburg in Meissen, where five experienced mine and melting workers assisted him. One year later, as Swedish troops advanced toward Saxony during the Great Northern War (1700-1721), the young alchemist was transferred to the heavily guarded Königstein Fortress in Dresden. After a peace treaty was signed in September 1707, he was brought back to the Venus Bastion in Dresden, having been unable to conduct a single experiment for over a year.

Under increasing pressure from Augustus the Strong, Böttger still could not deliver on his promise and even admitted this in writing to the king. This may have prompted Böttger to shift his focus from gold to porcelain, which may have appeared a more attainable goal. Porcelain was a common attribute in the Baroque households of the European aristocracy, used to display wealth and prestige, and Augustus the Strong showed a pronounced interest in it. To reduce the cost of this expensive interest, the king sought to establish local porcelain production and had already begun funding von Tschirnhaus's research several years prior. Moreover, he believed local production would enhance Saxony's image and prestige and become a major financial resource for the state, which was of considerable importance to the state.

Upon relocation to Venus Bastion, Böttger and his team initiated experiments to uncover the secret of porcelain production, supported by von Tschirnhaus, whose expertise encompassed kilns, lenses, and mirrors. Böttger diverged from his mentor's glass production focus, leveraging his own limited experience with ceramics. Within a remarkably short period of several months, he produced the first porcelain sample. This breakthrough was the result of systematic experimentation, where each stage's results informed the subsequent tests.[3] The team extensively studied chemical and physical processes, although a scientific explanation of the process would not emerge until the development of modern ceramic chemistry in the nineteenth century.

A laboratory protocol dated 15 January 1708 details the composition of hard-paste porcelain, often regarded as marking the successful production of European porcelain. This discovery was not immediately publicized due to concerns about the quality, stability, and glazing. Experiments continued until von Tschirnhaus's sudden death in October 1708. Three months later, Melchior Steinbrück (tutor of the von Tschirnhaus family) arrived in Dresden, and the work resumed. A week later, Böttger officially informed Augustus the Strong that he had discovered the formula for white porcelain and a red stoneware akin to porcelain.

He termed the latter *jasper porcelain*—after the opaque mineral jasper (speckled stone) used in jewellery—or *red porcelain*, now commonly known as *Böttger stoneware*. Similar red stoneware was already produced in China, Holland, and England; thus, the production process and ingredients were not entirely novel. However, Böttger's stoneware surpassed the existing varieties in quality due to its reduced porosity and increased hardness and density, achieved through higher firing temperatures.

During this experimental phase, predating the establishment of a manufactory, Chinese vessels and figurines were copied alongside the creation of new designs. For example, the Meissen archives indicate that sculptors Paul Heermann and Bernhard Miller each worked on three figurines in 1708.[4] The earliest known figurine, however, dates from 1709 and depicts Guanyin, an East Asian God of Mercy.

Böttger, hoping to be rewarded for his invention, requested his freedom from Augustus the Strong, but was instead told that he still had to produce gold first. Although he eventually regained his freedom in 1714, the promise Böttger made to Augustus the Strong as a 19-year-old in 1701 haunted him until his death 18 years later.

THE FOUNDATION OF THE MEISSEN MANUFACTORY AND THE BÖTTGER ERA: 1710–1717

Polish King and Saxon Elector Augustus the Strong invested heavily in porcelain research not solely for artistic reasons, but also because of the significant commercial potential he perceived.[5] Soon after Böttger's breakthrough, the Elector commissioned a team to assess the commercial viability of a porcelain manufactory. While Böttger's initial presentation in April 1709 failed to fully convince them, he provided more compelling evidence six months later. Consequently, on January 23, 1710, Augustus the Strong signed a Royal Decree, widely regarded as the establishment of the first European hard-paste porcelain manufactory.

This decree, published in Latin, French, German, and Dutch, held significant political weight beyond simply founding the Meissen manufactory. The invention of European porcelain was presented as evidence that Saxony and Poland had recovered from their defeat in the war with Sweden (1701-1706) and were once again at the forefront of European innovation.[6] Meissen porcelain would play a crucial role in Saxon foreign policy in the following decades, frequently serving as a diplomatic gift to other European courts.

The manufactory's first decade was marked by both practical difficulties and more fundamental structural problems. For instance, the Venus Bastion laboratory, the site of the initial experiments, proved inadequate for large-scale production, particularly in matters of security. This concerned not only kiln construction but also the safeguarding of the Arcanum, the closely guarded secret of the porcelain paste and enamel. Consequently, on March 7, 1710, the decision was made to relocate the entire operation to the Albrechtsburg in Meissen. However, it took six months for the new location to become fully operational, requiring the relocation of county administration and church leadership. This transition was not universally welcomed and may have contributed to tensions with parts of the Protestant population for years to come.

While formally appointed administrator, Böttger remained confined to the Venus Bastion in Dresden, limiting his visits to Meissen. A board of directors, headed by Michael Nehmitz, was therefore established to manage daily operations. Most of Böttger's former collaborators relocated to Meissen. Melchior Steinbrück, who had arrived in Dresden after von Tschirnhaus's death and married Böttger's sister, was appointed inspector of the manufactory.

In the manufactory's early years, production and sales focused on Böttger stoneware. By varying pastes and firing techniques, a range of colours—light red, dark red, brown, black, bluish, and even yellow—were achieved. A limited selection of glazes further diversified the stoneware. However, producing high-quality white porcelain proved more challenging than anticipated, and it wasn't until 1712 that it could be manufactured in larger quantities with fewer imperfections. The main issue wasn't the porcelain paste itself, but rather the glaze. This early *white porcelain* (now known as *Böttger porcelain*) consisted of three key ingredients: kaolin, alabaster (gypsum/calcium sulphate), and quartz. Alabaster was gradually replaced by feldspar in the early 1720s to eliminate the slightly yellowish tint.

Despite these advancements, porcelain production remained imperfect, with many pieces breaking during firing. Böttger continued his experiments to refine the manufacturing process, focusing on the paste, glaze, firing techniques, and kilns. Logistical challenges further complicated these efforts. More kilns were required to prevent production bottlenecks, and storage space was needed for the increasing inventory. Securing reliable supplies of high-quality kaolin and dry, easily split wood was also essential. Furthermore, the recruitment and extensive training of new employees significantly affected production quantity and quality.

Although a team assisted with the experiments, Böttger appears to have retained primary control over the full formulation—the *Arcanum*—for porcelain production. To safeguard this secret, he divided it into two parts. Michael Nehmitz received instructions for preparing the paste, while Bartelmei learned the glazing and firing processes. This division led to separate, isolated departments within the manufactory, creating inefficiencies. Moreover, while the initial preparation, shaping, and firing occurred in Meissen, the glazing, painting, gilding, and polishing were carried out in Dresden. This separation not only increased costs but also made the entire production process cumbersome. The lack of clear responsibilities between Böttger and Nehmitz, compounded by Böttger's infrequent trips to Meissen and declining health—largely due to chemical exposure and inadequate protection during experiments—likely contributed to these problems. This situation may have influenced the decision to restore his freedom in 1714.

These challenges were compounded by financial difficulties. Despite the demand for porcelain exceeding the supply, the enterprise consistently required financial support from the Saxon Elector. Management problems, including ambiguous decision-making structures, the absence of a clear pricing policy, and irrational expenses, further hampered progress. The fact that the bookkeeper was based in Dresden and rarely visited Meissen also had negative repercussions. Consequently, salaries were often paid months late, leading to employee dissatisfaction. This considerably increased the risk of skilled workers seeking better opportunities elsewhere and potentially sharing their expert knowledge with competitors.

Porcelain production required not only technical skill but also artistic expertise. Initially, Court Potter Fisher oversaw the creation of vessels, but Böttger was reportedly dissatisfied with his work.[7] In 1710, Court Goldsmith Johann Jacob Irminger (1635-1724) was employed and, two years later, became the head of the design department. While it may seem unusual that a goldsmith, rather than a potter, was chosen for this role, it is explained by the fact that metalwork, at the time, involved more artistic and decorative elements than ceramics. Most potters were primarily technical craftsmen, whereas artistically gifted individuals were typically involved with gold and silver.[8] Irminger not only created new shapes for tableware and table decorations but also taught and corrected the work of his colleagues. Initially, production focused on copying Chinese vessels and shapes. However, thanks to Irminger, a distinctly European porcelain style, often featuring floral motifs, began to develop.[9] Irminger typically created his models in silver or copper and then had them remodelled in Böttger stoneware. Over time, Irminger's interest in working for the Meissen manufactory waned. His relationship with the leadership deteriorated after Böttger's death in 1719, and he became increasingly absent until he finally resigned in 1720.[10]

Böttger stoneware decoration shared more similarities with glass and gemstone work than with ceramics. An initial technique involved polishing, sometimes combining polished and unpolished surfaces,[11] and mounting the stoneware with silver, bronze, or pewter, drawing on Irminger's experience as a smith. Polishing may have served both artistic and practical purposes, as the stoneware emerged from the kiln with a grey and matte surface that turned red upon polishing upon polishing.[12] Relief decorations were soon introduced, primarily using cutting and grinding. Another original decoration involved applying a black glaze, followed by etching a design. Gilding was also increasingly employed to accentuate the ornamentation. Creating paint that could withstand the high firing temperatures proved more challenging than producing porcelain itself. Consequently, a 'cold painting' technique was introduced in the early 1710s, where lacquer paint was used to decorate the porcelain without further firing. This method was less durable, with the paint often peeling or cracking, resulting in few surviving examples today. Much of this post-production processing occurred outside the Meissen manufactory, with independent glass cutters in Dresden, Meissen, and Bohemia handling the grinding and polishing.

White porcelain production reached a satisfactory level by 1712, leading to its sale the following year, particularly as it was cheaper to produce than Böttger stoneware.[13] This led to a relatively rapid decline in interest in stoneware. Production largely ceased around 1728, and the exact original formula was no longer preserved (the modern-day Böttgersteinzeug differs from the original). Initially, the same forms and moulds used for stoneware were adopted for white porcelain. However, this approach was unsuitable, as the thick porcelain glaze softened the sculptural elements and details. Consequently, Irminger designed new shapes, reducing the use of decorations like acanthus or laurel leaves. The decoration of porcelain mirrored that of stoneware, including metal or semi-precious stone mountings and the use of 'cold paint.'

Johann George Funcke, a Dresden goldsmith who frequently gilded and painted Böttger stoneware and white porcelain as an external artist, played an active role in experimenting with overglaze or enamel paint. Between 1713 and 1718, he successfully developed black, yellow, blue, green, light and dark purple paints, with Böttger adding another green and dark red to the palette.

Polychrome decorations were still a few years away, but the development of enamel colours enabled camaieu landscapes—decorations made in different tones of one colour through multiple layers, creating a more sculptural effect.

The search for underglaze paint was more challenging. After producing his first white porcelain, Böttger believed he would quickly replicate the cobalt blue underglaze decoration of Ming-period China. European ceramics like Delft faience and Hamburg stoneware had already found success with this technique. However, the high firing temperatures required for porcelain production caused the decoration's contours to blur, and the colour to change. Augustus the Strong offered 1000 Thalers to anyone who could invent a satisfactory blue paint. David Köhler, an arcanist and Böttger's collaborator since 1705, succeeded in 1717, developing a stable underglaze blue suitable for high-fired porcelain. In subsequent years, he and his colleagues refined the formula, realizing that replacing the alabaster in the porcelain paste with feldspar improved the paint's stability. A glaze that complemented the underglaze blue paint was not developed until 1733. As with other decorations, the underglaze paint was initially used to imitate Chinese porcelain. A decade later, a new décor for underglaze decoration emerged: the famous Bleu Onion pattern. A key difference between the Chinese and Meissen techniques was that in China, the blue paint was applied to dried porcelain, whereas in Meissen and other hard-paste porcelain manufactories, the object underwent a first firing before painting.

Production in the following years was primarily guided by the priorities of Augustus the Strong, the manufactory's patron and principal customer. Imitations of Asian porcelain were in high demand, reflecting its status as a primary point of reference for porcelain art and the widespread interest in Asia during the early 18th century. Consequently, many early *'Böttger porcelain'* figurines were copies of Chinese figures such as Guanyin and Confucius, as well as so-called *'pagodas'*, mirroring earlier models for Böttger stoneware.[14] This extended beyond vessels to include detailed statuettes of animals and pagodas. (While a pagoda is a temple structure, the term was also used to describe the idols, such as gods and Buddhas, worshipped within these buildings.[15]) Some of these porcelain pagodas featured nodding heads, moving hands, and tongues, while others functioned as incense burners, with smoke emanating from the ears and mouth.[16] The Meissen copies were slightly smaller than their Chinese counterparts, likely due to the use of plaster casts for creating moulds, with the subsequent sintering process causing an approximate 10% reduction in volume during firing.

However, not all products were mere copies. The manufactory's employees also exercised their creativity by inventing new forms, albeit heavily inspired by Chinese examples. New vessel forms and shapes were also created, based on models from silversmiths. Additionally, a limited number of new figurines and memorial coins (mainly moulded on the basis of silver coins) were produced during this first decade, almost all linked to five prominent Saxon sculptors of the time: Balthasar Permoser, Benjamin Thomae, Johann Kretzschmar, Paul Heermann, and Christian Kirchner. It remains unclear whether their contributions were voluntary or influenced by pressure from the Royal Court to contribute to the manufactory's success. Notably, in the early years, the term 'sculptor' was used for those who created new figurines; the term 'modeller' came into use later.[17] Many of the new objects were not mass-produced in moulds but were entirely modelled by hand, accounting for the slight size variations among surviving items.[18]

While it's uncertain whether the leading German Baroque sculptor Balthasar Permoser personally created anything in red stoneware or Böttger porcelain, he has been called the 'Father of the porcelain figurine.'[19] This designation stems not only from the fact that several of his ivory and wooden sculptures were replicated in stoneware and porcelain but also because his work represented a crucial preliminary stage in the development of porcelain figurative art.[20]

Benjamin Thomae, another early Meissen artist, modelled the 'Head of Persephone' and a crucifix in Böttger stoneware, as well as a 47 cm tall figurine of 'Johannes under the Cross' in Böttger porcelain.[21] He is mentioned once more in the archives in 1734, when he worked on a large tureen for Count Sułkowski's service.[22]

Johann Joachim Kretzschmar produced figurines of Augustus the Strong in both stoneware and porcelain.[23] Paul Heermann was known for his copies of works from antiquity, which explains the prevalence of antique heads like Apollo, Vitellius, and Proserpina among the earliest stoneware pieces. However, these were not exact copies, but rather new creations inspired by the originals, often influenced by Bernini, whose work Heermann knew well from his time in Rome.[24] Christian Kirchner created a 9 cm medal of Russian Tsar Peter the Great in Böttger stoneware around 1712,[25] and also produced several vases and a sphinx in Böttger porcelain.[26] Perhaps more significant than his own creations for the Meissen manufactory was his role in paving the way for his younger brother, Gottlieb Kirchner, to become the first in-house modeller at Meissen in 1727.

Around 1712, an important red stoneware creation featured six characters from the Italian Comedy, or Commedia dell'Arte. Stylistic analysis suggests that Permoser, Thomae, and Heermann each created two of these characters.[27] However, it is also likely that Permoser only made the wooden models for the figurines, with someone else sculpting them in red stoneware.[28] Paul Heermann's figurine of Pantalone was clearly inspired by an engraving from Robert Boissard's book *Mascarades*, published in 1597. The Commedia dell'Arte remained a popular theme in the following decades, inspiring both new figures and tableware designs.[29]

Independently of Böttger and von Tschirnhaus, French Jesuit missionary François Xavier d'Entrecolles learned how to manufacture porcelain in Jingdezhen (the *'Porcelain Capital'* of China). He engaged in this industrial spying by studying Chinese publications, observing the production process, and discussing it with Catholic converts working in the industry. In a letter to his superior in Paris in 1712, he explained the entire production process; the letter was published soon after. However, this publication did not simplify porcelain production or lead to a rapid proliferation of manufactories.

As part of a broader economic policy aimed at reducing imports and dependence on foreign nations, the Prussians also sought to uncover the secret of porcelain production.[30] Plaue an der Havel already possessed a ceramics industry, owing to the region's plentiful supply of high-quality red clay. In 1713, upon learning of Meissen's success and achieving preliminary results in stoneware and porcelain experimentation, the Prussian bureaucrat Friedrich von Görne established a manufactory in Plaue.[31] The Saxon authorities responded proactively by dispatching spies to Plaue an der Havel to gain insight into their competitor's operations.[32] Although the Plaue factory managed to produce items superficially similar to Böttger's red stoneware, it never presented a significant threat to the Meissen manufactory and was shut down a decade later. Nonetheless, this situation was detrimental to Böttger's reputation with Augustus the Strong, demonstrating that espionage by other European courts was yielding results and necessitating stricter security measures at the Meissen manufactory.

In 1717, Claudius Innocentius Du Paquier established a porcelain factory in Vienna, Austria. Despite his knowledge of chemistry and information gleaned from d'Entrecolles' published accounts, he struggled to achieve tangible results. Consequently, he sought to entice workers from Meissen. With the assistance of an Austrian diplomat in Poland-Saxony, he recruited Christoph Conrad Hunger, an enameler and gilder, to Vienna in 1717, followed by the arcanist Samuel Stölzel two years later. Both had been assistants to Böttger since 1705 and brought with them not only the secret formula for the porcelain paste but also kiln designs. Despite a prohibition on sales to entities other than the Meissen manufactory, they managed to obtain kaolin from Aue, and by April 1719, a fully functional porcelain production was underway in Vienna. However, this collaboration proved short-lived, as the Vienna Porcelain Manufactory failed to deliver on its promise of substantial financial compensation. Stölzel returned to Meissen, and Hunger relocated to Venice, where, with three other investors, he founded the Venice Porcelain Manufactory. Hunger departed Venice in 1724 and returned to the Meissen manufactory in 1727 as a gilder. He soon left again, serving as director of the Rör-strand Porcelain Factory in Stockholm (1729-33), unsuccessfully attempting to establish a manufactory in Denmark in 1737, and playing a crucial role in the founding of the Imperial Porcelain Factory in St. Petersburg in 1744. Many other European manufactories in the first half of the 18th century were established by or with the assistance of former Meissen employees.

On March 13, 1719, Böttger died at the age of 37, following years of illness exacerbated by exposure to fumes during his experiments, as well as alleged excessive smoking and alcohol consumption. Sadly, he never witnessed the Meissen manufactory achieve sound financial footing. After his death, a new commission was appointed to manage the manufactory, with Steinbrück named chief administrator. Several reforms were implemented, particularly considering the Vienna manufactory emerging as a major competitor. Salaries were increased, new kilns were commissioned, and a glaze mill was installed. These measures were followed by a marked improvement in the manufactory's finances by 1720, eliminating the need for court subsidies. This marked the end of the experimental phase and the beginning of a more structured period of artistic and commercial development.

HÖROLDT ERA: 1720 – 1731

The period from 1720 to 1731 is sometimes referred to as the *'Painting Period'* due to the Meissen manufactory's focus on painted decoration. The departure of Irminger and the arrival of the painter Johann Gregor Höroldt (1696-1775) in 1720 initiated a significant shift: the emphasis on sculpture diminished in favour of painted decoration on simpler forms. This trend continued for a decade until the arrival of the modeller Johann Joachim Kändler (1706-1775), who revitalized the sculptural dimension.[33] The relatively limited number of new sculptural models produced during this period suggests a reduced emphasis on formal innovation.

One of the main challenges during the Böttger era had been the lack of skilled labour, especially in painting. However, this changed with the arrival of Johann Gregor Höroldt. This development was made possible by Samuel Stölzel, Böttger's assistant, who had left Meissen in 1719 and aided in establishing a rival producer in Austria. When Stölzel returned to Meissen a year later, he brought with him Johann Gregor Höroldt, a painter from the Vienna Porcelain Manufactory familiar with a more vibrant palette and the style of Claudius du Paquier, the founder of the Vienna manufactory known for his distinct late Baroque designs.[34]

Although Höroldt became the manufactory's leading painter, he was supported by a team of painters who initially worked closely from his models and examples, with limited scope for individual stylistic expression.[35] Most of these painters had previously worked in the faience factory in Dresden, bringing relevant experience. Gradually, especially from the 1730s onward, Höroldt allowed the most talented painters—among them Heintze, Herold, Horn, Stadler, and von Löwenfinck—to develop more individual styles, provided they remained within the established character of Meissen painting.[36] During this time, buyers generally showed little interest in the identity of individual painters, so they remained anonymous. Although identifying individual painters is often difficult, if not impossible, it has been the subject of much research.[37] For instance, Johann Ehrenfried Stadler and Johann Christoph Horn specialized in Japanese-style decoration and floral motifs, while Johann Georg Heintze focused on landscapes and figures, Johann Gottlieb Klinger on flowers, and Christian Friedrich Herold on harbour scenes and, later, flowers.

While Höroldt's team produced much of Meissen porcelain's painted decoration, independent painters also contributed from their own workshops. The Seuter and Auffenwerth families of Augsburg were particularly active in this regard.[38] Augsburg had become a goldsmithing centre around 1700, fostering a strong tradition of family firms painting faience. This tradition helps explain why porcelain blanks were decorated with gold and silver and, in later stages, painted, in Augsburg, a city 400 km southwest of Meissen. These Augsburg gold decorations peaked between 1725 and 1735.[39]

Despite its leading position, the Meissen manufactory continued to pursue technical improvements in both paste and decoration. From the early 1720s, feldspar replaced alabaster in the porcelain paste, improving paint adhesion and resulting in a whiter, less yellow-toned porcelain body. While advancements were made in enamel and firing processes, the 1720s saw improvements primarily driven by new artistic trends, particularly in painting. Because of the instability of the paints, the final colours after firing were often unpredictable. The initial limited palette of colours expanded over the following years. As Höroldt initially lacked experience in paint production, he relied on materials supplied by David Köhler and Samuel Stölzel. After Köhler's death in 1723, a book containing 82 pages of recipes was discovered, though nine pages were missing. Over the next eight years, Höroldt developed 16 new enamel paints, enabling the creation of novel painting motifs. Many of these motifs are recorded in the 124-page Schulz Codex, a compilation of painted motifs and decorative designs, acquired in the early 20th century by the collector Georg Wilhelm Schulz.[40]

The development of the first cobalt blue underglaze paint by David Köhler was particularly significant because creating a paint that could withstand temperatures exceeding 1400 degrees Celsius was a considerable challenge. This innovation enabled the manufactory to compete with Chinese blue-and-white porcelain and faience from Delft. Around 1728, Johann David Kretschman, a painter at the manufactory, created the famous Blue Onion pattern, refining it throughout the next decade. Initially known as 'Bleu ordinaire' and 'Blau und Weiss ordinair gemahlt,' the pattern drew inspiration from a Chinese design featuring peaches, pomegranates, and lemons. The pomegranate motif is traditionally said to have been interpreted at Meissen as an onion, hence the pattern's name. The use of cobalt blue also made it possible to apply the crossed swords mark in underglaze blue in 1722, which became a systematic practice around 1725 at the suggestion of manufactory inspector Melchior Steinbrück. The purpose was to distinguish Meissen products. The logo was inspired by the Coat of Arms of the Saxon Electorate, and although this trademark has evolved over the past three centuries, its foundation remains the Crossed Swords.

Initially, Höroldt worked from Chinese and Japanese models, as these were highly fashionable in Europe. This strategy aimed to reduce expensive imports and generate income for the Saxon state.[41] Subsequently, he adopted a more creative approach to decoration, developing his own patterns featuring flowers, landscapes, mythological animals, and invented East Asian scenes, such as the *'yellow lion,'* *'red dragon,'* *'three friends,'* or *'chrysanthemum and butterfly.'*[42] In these East Asian scenes, he created novel combinations of dragons, phoenixes, butterflies, insects, and other elements that appealed to Europeans, even though they lacked coherence within Chinese or Japanese symbolism and were not well understood in Europe.[43] For instance, Höroldt likely did not know that, according to East Asian symbolism, his *'yellow lion'* pattern would represent a marriage proposal.[44]

One of Höroldt's specialties was *chinoiseries*, which were not direct copies of Chinese or Japanese designs. Instead, they reflected Chinese artistic influences by either imitating East Asian motifs or expressing European perceptions of Chinese and Japanese life. Although such paintings with gold etching may have originated during Böttger's time or in the years immediately following his death, Höroldt appears to have brought this style to a particularly mature form. These chinoiseries, however, were not unique to Meissen but were part of a broader artistic trend across Europe.

Around the mid-1720s, Baroque influences became apparent in the manufactory's artistic output, with European scenes gaining prominence. These compositions frequently depicted Dutch landscapes, harbour views with European and Ottoman merchants, hunting and battle scenes, and *Watteau* scenes.[45] The *Watteau* scenes, named for their inspiration from the paintings and engravings of French painter Jean-Antoine Watteau, typically portrayed lovers, musicians, and theatre players in park settings. These scenes were often created by borrowing individual figures or couples from Watteau's works and placing them in newly composed settings. However, the manufactory also drew inspiration from the works of other artists, such as Nicolas Lancret and Jacopo Amiconi.

As previously mentioned, the emphasis shifted from sculptural elements to painted decoration. The manufactory concentrated on producing tableware with simple designs and reproducing existing figurines, while still emphasizing East Asian forms and patterns. New figurines were also created using models purchased from sculptors in Saxony and southern Germany. For instance, in 1725, the manufactory acquired 161 plaster models, most of which were reproduced in porcelain in the subsequent months and years.[46] These small porcelain figurines served as durable substitutes for earlier table decorations made from sugar and gum tragacanth, adorning banquet tables and entertaining guests during lengthy royal banquets.[47] Confectioners had long used similar decorations for centrepieces during medieval times to distract the guests during lengthy royal banquets.[48] The painted embellishments on these small porcelain figurines in the 1720s primarily served to accentuate selected sculptural details. The more than 50 different dwarf figurines, many of them derived from engravings by French Baroque printmaker Jacques Callot, proved especially popular during this period. Though they were likely not conceived as a collection, the figurines varied in size and plinth design. Dwarfs, particularly those riding horses, also became a popular motif for decorating plates, cups, and teapots.[49]

The limited sculptural innovation in Meissen porcelain may stem not from a lack of creativity among the manufactory's employees, but rather from the personal preferences of Augustus the Strong, its most significant patron.[50] From 1719 to 1733, he purchased an estimated 43% of Meissen's total production.[51] The Saxon Elector and King of Poland, deeply engaged with porcelain collecting, conceived the idea around 1727 of a Porcelain Palace, envisioned as a Versailles-style display of wealth. Dissatisfied with more conventional porcelain, his ambition was to surpass Chinese and Japanese artistry by creating large, lavishly decorated objects. He selected the Dutch Palace in Dresden as the location, as it already housed his art collection since 1717,[52] and subsequently expanded and renamed it the Japanese Palace. The ground floor was intended to exhibit East Asian porcelain, while the upper floor would showcase domestic Meissen production. The Palace was not only to display the Elector's wealth and artistic taste but also to demonstrate Saxony's economic superiority.[53] However, the reconstruction and furnishing of the Palace with porcelain remained incomplete when Augustus the Strong died in 1733. Although his son, Augustus III, continued the project, the Japanese Palace never functioned as a museum for porcelain art, and the endeavour was abandoned in 1740. Today, the Dresden Porcelain Collection comprises some 20,000 items, only a tenth of which are exhibited in the Zwinger Palace in Dresden.

The grand central hall on the upper floor of the Japanese Palace was planned to house 296 porcelain mammals and 297 birds, most rendered in life-size. This collection encompassed not only domestic (e.g., goat, dog, fox, squirrel) and exotic animals (e.g., lion, rhinoceros, monkey) but also three mythological creatures (i.e., dragon, sphinx, and unicorn).[54] This ambitious display can be understood within the broader context of royal interest in animals, paralleling their hunting pursuits, menageries, and cabinets of curiosities featuring stuffed animals. The surrounding rooms were intended to be filled with thousands of other exquisitely decorated and gilded porcelain objects.

As the need for a sculptor to oversee the sculptural aspects of new porcelain creations grew, the manufactory recruited Johann Gottlieb Kirchner (1706-1768) in 1727. The 21-year-old wood sculptor was the younger brother of Christian Kirchner, who had provided models some fifteen years prior. Kirchner's arrival at Meissen marked the end of occasional contributions from independent sculptors. However, he was dismissed after only a year due to frequent illness and absences. He also reportedly struggled with insecurity and adapting to the unique properties of porcelain.[55] Porcelain differs significantly from other materials, as it can shrink by up to 16% during firing and the glaze tends to soften contours. This requires the modeller to compensate by exaggerating details. This technical challenge was particularly pronounced for large animal sculptures, as there were few relevant precedents for such large-scale porcelain animal sculptures available to Meissen's modellers. Overcoming this hurdle necessitated improvements in glaze, kilns, porcelain paste composition, and calculations of optimal firing duration. The ambition to create large porcelain objects spurred new developments in porcelain production and artistry. While Kirchner produced impressive works, the lack of documentation makes attribution difficult. He is known to have created clocks[56] and a candlestick, but most notably, a *'Temple of Venus'* inspired by the Nymph Bath Fountain at the Zwinger Palace in Dresden. The Temple of Venus mirrored the fountain's architecture with similar columns and niches, and the figurine of Venus was a smaller version of the statue in Dresden, flanked by Juno and Mars, with a pedestal decorated with chinoiseries.

Johann Christoph Ludwig Lücke, an ivory carver, filled the vacant post of modeller in March or April 1728. However, he met a similar fate to his predecessor in less than a year. It is unclear whether he was dismissed or left voluntarily, but Meissen archives indicate he was frequently absent, rarely worked, failed to instruct students, and was even accused of insulting and physically assaulting a colleague.[57] Besides a figurine of Augustus the Strong, he produced goblets and jewellery.[58]

This growing demand for large-scale sculptural works marked a shift in priorities, preparing the ground for the reintroduction of a dedicated modeller. Against this background, Kirchner was re-hired in 1730 to address the manufactory's need for a modeller capable of executing Augustus the Strong's large-scale commissions.

HÖROLDT-KÄNDLER ERA: 1731 – 1756

The 1730s were a relatively peaceful and economically stable period. However, the First and Second Silesian Wars (1740-42 and 1744-45) between Prussia and Austria significantly impacted Saxony, given its geographical position between these two powers. These conflicts had considerable economic consequences and directly affected the manufactory's operations. For instance, in the second half of December 1744, the city of Meissen was directly affected by military operations. Anticipating this, the manufactory closed three days prior, with employees deliberately destroying selected equipment, hiding paste and enamel ingredients, and relocating key personnel to Dresden to prevent the Prussians from obtaining the Arcanum or otherwise acquiring the technological knowledge.[59] Following the Battle of Kesselsdorf in December 1745, approximately 25 km southeast of Meissen, the Albrechtsburg served as a military hospital for six months.[60] Part of the stock was confiscated and sent to the Prussian King Frederick the Great, and firewood was seized by occupying forces. Saxony recovered relatively quickly from the Second Silesian War, and the Meissen manufactory expanded steadily, employing 378 people in 1750 compared to only 100 approximately 20 years prior.[61]

While these political and economic disruptions affected the manufactory, its principal developments were driven by other factors. The demand for expensive porcelain, technological advancements in the production process, and the presence of skilled craftsmen led to the manufactory's international reputation and the creation of a distinctively European porcelain style. During a period when many new porcelain manufactories emerged (e.g., Vincennes in 1740, Chelsea in 1743, Mennecy in 1745, Höchst in 1746, Fürstenberg and Nymphenburg in 1747, Berlin in 1751, Copenhagen and Frankenthal in 1755), the Meissen manufactory did not initially experience competition of equal standing because it aimed for and succeeded in delivering a particularly high level of luxury craftmanship. Most other manufactories primarily copied Meissen objects or followed its style. Although some achieved high standards of porcelain art, few, if any, appear to have surpassed Meissen in prestige during this period, especially since many only produced soft-paste porcelain (e.g., Chantilly, Mennecy, Vincennes, Chelsea, Bow).

In 1731, Augustus the Strong decided to become more personally involved in managing the Meissen manufactory. He took this step after concluding that his interests were insufficiently represented and that reforms were needed to ensure the manufactory's financial sustainability. The manufactory director, Count Carl Heinrich von Hoym, had engaged in irregular and, at times, dishonest practices, including producing imitations of East Asian porcelain, misappropriating funds, delaying the King's orders, and allegedly plotting to steal the Arcanum. The manufactory also continued to face production challenges; for example, firing large pieces remained problematic, often resulting in cracking, and the colours and glaze were not yet perfect. Improvements to the glaze composition in 1732/33 and 1739, for instance, reduced misfiring.[62] Even in later periods, producing large works remained a significant challenge; for example, the firing of the 1.8-meter-tall statue *Saxonia* in 2014 remained technically uncertain.

Augustus the Strong prioritized the implementation of his porcelain palace, requiring Johann Gottlieb Kirchner to focus on this task upon his return to Meissen in 1730. However, Kirchner's work pace was deemed too slow to meet the high production volume required, necessitating the recruitment of an additional modeller. In 1731, Johann Joachim Kändler (1706-1775), a wood and stone sculptor, joined Kirchner. Kirchner was given the title of Model Master and made Kändler's hierarchical superior. Kändler, the son of a pastor, had studied and worked under the guidance of two leading Saxon sculptors of the early 18th century. From 1718 to 1723, he worked with Johann Christian Feige, who primarily produced tombstones for the bourgeoisie and altars and figurines for churches. Evidence suggests that Feige and Kändler also collaborated on the construction of the Zwinger palace.[63]

From 1723, Kändler studied and worked with Benjamin Thomae, a renowned Saxon sculptor who had created models for the Meissen manufactory in the 1710s. Thomae and Kändler collaborated on renovations to the Green Vault, a palace transformed by the Elector-King into a public museum for state treasures. It is therefore likely that Augustus the Strong recognized Kändler's talent there and offered him the opportunity to work with porcelain at the manufactory.

Fuelled by Augustus the Strong's ambitious plans and the prevailing Baroque style in Saxony, Kirchner and Kändler were commissioned to produce a vast number of large-scale objects for the Japanese Palace, with the creation of animal figurines as the most significant task. In contrast to the highly stylized Asian porcelain animal figurines, the Meissen modellers aimed for a more naturalistic representation. This shift may reflect broader developments in zoological knowledge during that era, fostering a more informed understanding of the animal kingdom.[64]

The initial concept involved painting these large animals in their natural colours. However, the complex production process of such large-scale figures led to frequent cracking after the first firing. The risk of complete destruction during a second firing was deemed too high.[65] Consequently, cracks were typically filled with a mixture of sawdust and gypsum, coated with varnish, and occasionally decorated with cold paint.[66] This oil paint, applied atop the glaze without further firing, tended to flake off over time. As a result, surviving painted animals are often almost entirely white or exhibit darkened oil paint.

Despite his initial unfamiliarity with porcelain, Kändler demonstrated a strong aptitude for the material, adapting to it far more quickly than Kirchner. He reportedly impressed his colleagues by producing three models during his first week at the Meissen manufactory. However, the technical challenges of large-scale porcelain production remained only partially resolved.

The working relationship between Kändler and Kirchner was fraught with tension, exacerbated by Kirchner's displeasure at his subordinate receiving a higher salary. Following the denial of his request to equalize their compensation and also motivated by his preference for working with stone, Kirchner resigned in 1733, paving the way for Kändler to become the new Model Master.[67] Confidence in Kändler was sufficiently high that no additional modeller was recruited. In 1734 alone, he produced 39 large animals and 50 birds. Interestingly, Kirchner's name appears once more in a report from March 1737, documenting his delivery of two small figurines.[68]

Although Kirchner's work may appear less lifelike by comparison with Kändler, it should not be underestimated. Lacking a predecessor, he established a foundational body of knowledge and expertise upon which Kändler could build. He can be credited with creating the first large figurines—including an elephant, rhinoceros, lion, bear, leopard, lynx, monkey, foo dog, and several birds—as well as a number of vases (composed of several parts assembled with gold-plated bronze) exceeding one meter in height, and a 97 cm statue of the Apostle Paul. Kirchner appears to have developed an understanding of porcelain's specific qualities, evident in his smaller works, such as a Harlequin or the sculptural decorations for table sets or clock cases.[69]

Kirchner and Kändler possessed distinctly different styles. Kirchner's models resemble statues, portraying animals as typical or idealized representations.[70] The figurines are comparatively rough and less detailed. Kändler, in contrast, is more detailed and differentiated. He typically depicts animals in dynamic, naturalistic poses, as if in motion—for example, a parrot descending or an eagle consuming a fish. To achieve this realism, Kändler appears to have relied more on direct observation in nature, museums, or zoos rather than on pictorial sources. Augustus' interest in exotic animals contributed to efforts to acquire exotic specimens, including expeditions to Africa (1730–33), allowing Kändler and his colleagues to study not only European fauna. A notable example is Clara, a female Indian rhinoceros who toured Europe for 17 years and posed for Kändler in Dresden in 1747. Her depiction reveals significant differences from Kirchner's 1732 rhinoceros, which was based on Albrecht Dürer's famous woodcut.

Following the death of Augustus the Strong in 1733 and the accession of his son Augustus III, the manufactory entered a new phase marked by administrative and artistic changes. Primarily interested in hunting, paintings, and music, the new Saxon Elector and King of Poland delegated the governance of his country and the management of the manufactory to Prime Minister Count von Brühl (1700-1763), in whom he placed considerable trust. While Augustus III did not share his father's passion for porcelain, he recognized the enterprise's importance and prestige and initially insisted on continuing the works for the Japanese Palace.[71] After the delivery of 35,798 porcelain objects,[72] the project was abandoned around 1740. Nevertheless, the Meissen manufactory sustained its production of both tableware sets and fine art.

The quality of the works improved further, and the Meissen manufactory strengthened its leading position in the porcelain world. This success was not necessarily the result of harmonious collaboration between the different departments and artists within the workshop, but rather of the competition between modellers and painters. While Kändler's impressive work was a major step forward for the manufactory, Höroldt may have perceived a threat in this new colleague who would compete for fame and recognition. Höroldt and his painters believed that the beauty of porcelain lay in the painting, making the modelling secondary.

Kändler and the other modellers held the opposite view. Until Kändler's arrival, the emphasis was on the painting, and the forms were often simple. However, as the Baroque style gained prominence, the form, with its ornamentations, began to play a more significant role. This tension reflects a broader structural duality within the manufactory: that between sculptural invention and painterly refinement. The competition between modellers and painters spurred creativity and innovation on both sides, as best illustrated in the tableware. In many cases, the shape of these items was so dominant that the painters could hardly add anything, reducing their contribution at times to a form of ornamental embellishment. The Snowball Blossom Service and the Swan Service, described in more detail later in this chapter, exemplify this dynamic. Over time, however, and especially as simpler versions of tableware became more popular, painters were again able to showcase their mastery. The manufactory experienced some of its most artistically productive moments during this period, and much of the tableware and fine art modelled then continue to enjoy considerable popularity. Höroldt's contributions were also crucial to the development of European porcelain art. He established the foundation for the painting style and transformed the white porcelain into works of art through his decoration with bright Meissen colours,[73] which set an example for other manufactories throughout Europe.

After the Meissen manufactory reached its peak, the influence of both Kändler and Höroldt gradually decreased from 1750 onwards. Although they remained for more than a decade, they had to make way for new artists with new artistic influences. The market demanded less artistic imagination and preferred three-dimensional porcelain creations based on watercolours provided by merchants.[74]

Under von Brühl's leadership, the Meissen manufactory strengthened its financial position, developed its artistic direction, and gradually moved away from imitating the Chinese style, favouring more European forms for vessels and tableware. As interest in the Japanese Palace waned, the focus shifted from large-scale animal creations to smaller ones in the mid-1730s, followed by the production of figurines beyond animals in subsequent years, which will be discussed in detail later in this chapter. Given France's leading cultural role in Europe, the rise of the Rococo style in the 1730s significantly influenced the Meissen manufactory.[75] This influence was amplified by the fact that a large portion of sales went to Western Europe, necessitating adaptation to client tastes. The Rococo style, characterized by asymmetry, curved lines, and playfulness, ideally suited porcelain for creating artistic objects.[76] Rococo figurines, being much smaller than the monumental Baroque creations, required a different production approach.

Johann Joachim Kändler is generally regarded as the most influential modeller in the history of the Meissen manufactory. He aimed to diversify the use of the material, producing not only figurines and tableware but also bells, clocks, lanterns, shirt buttons, key rings, needle cases, cane handles, and various other practical items. Kändler shared with Augustus the Strong an exceptionally ambitious vision for porcelain, not only in terms of quality but also of scale and quantity. While many of his contemporaries remained cautious, he pursued large-scale works with notable determination, often testing the technical limits of the material. He appears to have believed that almost any form could be realized in porcelain, even if it required assembling multiple pieces.[77] In this sense, his thinking aligned with the principles of Baroque art, where exaggeration and grandeur were fundamental. It is also important to note Kändler's extensive use of mythology in his work, a subject he had studied with his father and continued to pursue through private classes with M. Weiss during his time at the Meissen manufactory.

One example of his ambitious vision is his trip to Paris in 1750, where Kändler intended to present a gift for the birth of the first child of Maria Josepha, daughter of Augustus III, and French crown prince Louis.[78] This gift was a three-meter-high creation consisting of a porcelain console table topped with a huge mirror surrounded by rocaille ornamentation, flower tendrils, and figurines of Apollo and the nine muses. The latter were likely based on figurines already created for Friedrich II the Great of Prussia.[79] The object was later destroyed during the French Revolution, and no traces remain of a copy made for the 1900 Paris Exhibition.[80]

Even more ambitious was the creation of a 10-meter high equestrian statue of Augustus III. Kändler began developing this ambitious concept as early as 1734,[81] creating several smaller figurines of Augustus III on horseback in the years that followed. However, it was only after almost two decades of discussion that a formal order was placed in 1751 to create this ambitious Baroque project. Led by Kändler, a team of sculptors and carpenters began working on the statue, which was designed to be assembled from numerous pieces. This project was largely a personal endeavour for Kändler, separate from the manufactory's regular work; consequently, the statue was constructed in a separate building, not within the Albrechtsburg. In 1753, Kändler created a 123 cm model to give the King an idea of the final product. This model, originally housed in the Japanese Palace, is now part of the Dresden Porcelain Collection. The full-sized statue was never completed due to several factors: financial difficulties resulting from the Third Silesian War, the manufactory's control falling to the Prussian King Friedrich, and Kändler's strained relationship with the manufactory administration.[82] Ultimately, this project resulted in significant financial losses for Kändler, who had personally pre-financed a large portion of the work and workers for five years and was never reimbursed.[83]

During his 34 years at the Meissen manufactory, Johann Joachim Kändler is estimated to have created over 2,000 distinct models of animals, groups, and people. Such a vast output would not have been possible without the support of his colleagues. Several assistants were recruited to support the Model Master, including Johann Friedrich Eberlein, Friedrich Elias Meyer, Johan Gottlieb Ehder, and Peter Reinicke. These assistants prepared works for

Kändler's correction and improvement, as well as creating and copying moulds. Effective collaboration required that these assistants share a similar approach to the work and style as Kändler. Archival records allow us to trace the involvement of these assistants in many works. However, many of them also created entire figurines independently. For example, Eberlein created numerous apostles, saints, and other figurines. His personal style, slightly different from Kändler's, is characterized by stronger stylization, sharp faces, pulled-down noses, sharp chins, and an inclined position of the eyes.[84] Meyer's works are recognizable by their slim bodies and proportionally small, similar-looking faces.[85] Much younger than the others, Meyer appears not to have been significantly influenced by the Baroque style. Instead, he worked fully in the Rococo spirit with its typical asymmetry. He may also have introduced the rocaille motif to the figurines' pedestals in 1748; from 1731 until then, the pedestals had been cubical or amorphous-naturalistic.[86]

In the early 1730s, Meissen introduced another innovation: some of the first comprehensive tableware services in Europe. Previously, production had been limited to individual plates and vessels. This shift coincided with the growing popularity of coffee, tea, and chocolate among European elites, necessitating the creation of suitable cups. Porcelain proved particularly well suited for these hot beverages due to its heat resistance. While Chinese and Japanese porcelain manufacturers had not adapted in the same way to evolving European dining practices in the 17th and early 18th centuries, European producers developed porcelain as a substitute for metal tableware. Initially, they emulated metal designs, as seen in the Sułkowski Service (1735-36). However, a distinct porcelain aesthetic gradually emerged.

Johann Joachim Kändler's first complete set was a dinner service created in 1731 for Count Friesen, the husband of Augustus the Strong's illegitimate daughter. The output of tableware services, each with unique forms and shapes, was remarkable: 35 services by 1736, and another 47 in the following decade. Throughout the

1730s, royal houses and aristocratic families commissioned most of these services to display their wealth and social standing. A Meissen service, especially one bearing a family coat of arms, became a coveted status symbol.[87] Notable patrons included Augustus the Strong, Swedish King Adolf Frederik I, Sardinian King Victor Amadeus II, and Russian General Field Marshal von Münnich. By the 1740s, the clientele for these services expanded to include wealthier members of the bourgeoisie.[88]

Although not intended for mass production, several services achieved considerable success, including the *'Old Ozier'* (based on the Sułkowski set) and the Brandenstein, Dulong, and Marseille sets. The *'New Cutout'* (Neuer Ausschnitt) of 1745 became the most famous pattern.[89] It eventually comprised one of the largest ranges of individual items (i.e. 550) and even inspired Zepner's *'Large Cutout'* in 1973. During the period 1746–1756, tableware design diverged along class lines. The aristocracy favoured the ornate Rococo style, while the bourgeoisie preferred a simpler, more naturalistic aesthetic.

While all of these services represent significant artistic achievements, the following section examines four in greater detail.

The most renowned service created at Meissen is generally considered the Swan Service, modelled between 1737 and 1742 at the behest of Count Heinrich von Brühl. He commissioned a spectacular table service to support his representational role at the Saxon court, particularly in hosting official banquets in his capacity as Prime Minister,[90] given Augustus III's limited direct involvement in government administration. Kändler, assisted by Ehder, Eberlein, and several other formers and bosserers, designed and produced approximately 2,200 objects, sufficient to serve over 100 guests.

The precise inspiration for Kändler's specific form and relief remains unclear. One interpretation suggests that water was selected as the central theme due to the name Brühl meaning *'damp place.'*[91] Von Brühl reportedly reviewed at least 18 different plate design samples, ultimately choosing the one inspired by a shell and decorated with a relief of swans and herons in the background. Stylistically, the Swan Service is notable, illustrating the transition from the late Baroque to the Rococo style through the use of the shell motif even before the *rocaille* style was fully established in France.[92] Kändler had previously used the shell motif in a washbowl in 1728,[93] likely because it was a popular design element in 18th-century Dresden, frequently used in water fountains.[94] The increasing use of shells and other rocaille motifs in the mid-18th century coincided with the rise of Rococo as the dominant artistic trend in Europe. The swan relief itself was based on a 1658 copper engraving by Bohemian artist Václav Hollar, who drew inspiration from a drawing by Francis Barlow.[95]

Beyond the recurring swans and herons, the service also features other real and mythological aquatic animals. The modeller appears to have approached the task with particular care, spending three days studying shells in a museum to enhance the service's naturalism.[96] Some objects within the service extended beyond purely functional purposes, serving as fine art pieces linked to aquatic mythology. For example, several objects are modelled in the form of a swan, and two confectionery stands were created, one with Glaukos and the other with a Nereid mermaid as a base. Glaukos was a mortal fisherman who gained immortality and became a sea-god after consuming a magical herb. The Nereids were traditionally counted as fifty sea nymphs who accompanied Poseidon, the God of the Sea, and protected sailors and fishermen. The largest soup tureens and their lids were adorned with figurines from the story of the Nereid Galatea. One scene depicts Galatea and Amor on a dolphin, another shows Venus in a shell pulled by swans, and yet another portrays Galatea together with Venus. Kändler was likely influenced by Francesco Albani's painting of Galatea, which was on display in the Dresden Gallery. This table service exemplifies the competition between Kändler's and Höroldt's teams, as the relief's pronounced sculptural quality left little scope for painted decoration. Aside from a gilded border, the service features only so-called *'Indian flowers'* motifs and the coat of arms of the von Brühl-Kolowrat family.

The second most extensive set of tableware from this period was the Sułkowski service. Designed in the Baroque style for Alexander Joseph von Sułkowski—allegedly an illegitimate son of Augustus the Strong and later Prime Minister under Augustus III—it served as the basis for the popular Ozier pattern. Sułkowski was also in charge of managing the Elector's treasures, including his porcelain collection.

The *'Gotzkowsky's Flowers in Relief'* Service, created between 1741 and 1744 through close collaboration between Kändler, Eberlein, and Ehder, was based on the relief of silver Baroque vessels.[97] This design became a model for tableware at numerous other royal courts. For instance, the Green Watteau Service adopted the same form and was decorated with Watteau scenes in copper green camaieu-painting. The Elisabeth Service (for Russian Tsarina Elisabeth) and the St Andrew Service also utilized this design. The plates feature two branches with flowers in the centre, forming an almost complete circle. The border is divided into four larger and four smaller sections, with the larger sections adorned with a flowering branch. The original extent of painted decoration on the service remains uncertain, as no securely identified examples are known to have survived. A large centrepiece depicting Mount Parnassus and the nine muses, along with a figurine of Pallas, were created as additional table decorations. Despite the service's name, it is more likely that Johann Gotzkowsky ordered it on behalf of the Prussian King Frederick the Great,[98] rather than owning it himself. Johann Ernst Gotzkowsky played a significant role in the development of porcelain production in Prussia. In 1761, he established a new porcelain manufactory in Berlin and appointed Friedrich Elias Meyer as chief modeller. Two years later, King Friedrich II acquired the manufactory and transformed it into the Royal Porcelain Manufactory in Berlin (KPM), which remains in operation today.

The Snowball Blossom Service (also known as *'Boule de neige'*) offers a fourth example of tableware from this era. This coffee set, created in 1739 for Electress Maria Josepha (for whom a total of four services were made), is often regarded as one of the most artistically refined coffee sets produced by the Meissen manufactory. However, its delicate ornamentation indicates that its decorative function clearly outweighed its practical use. The snowball blossom motif was later adapted for other creations, such as vases. The motif continued to inspire later designers; for example, Paul Scheurich drew inspiration from these blossoms for a new vase design, and Meissen jewellery also found inspiration in them, as discussed in a later chapter.

While three-dimensional modelling became a dominant aspect of tableware and figurines, painting and decorative development remained central to production at Meissen. In the 1730s, the Kakiemon style gained considerable popularity. This decorative style originated in the region of Arita, Japan (a Meissen sister city since 1979), and is named after Sakaida Kakiemon, the potter traditionally credited with developing overglaze enamel decoration on porcelain in Japan during the first half of the 17th century. Kakiemon designs typically cover about a third of the porcelain surface and feature symbolic motifs such as flowers, birds, dragons, bamboo, and pines. For example, peach or plum blossoms are often associated with youth and female beauty, while the lotus represents fertility and rejuvenation. Augustus the Strong, a collector of Japanese Kakiemon porcelain, commissioned the Meissen manufactory to produce imitations.

However, the Meissen painters did not simply copy these Japanese designs; they gradually developed their own décors inspired by the Kakiemon style. Chinese designs were copied less frequently, as the Japanese style more closely aligned with European tastes at the time.[99] The *'Yellow Lion'* and *'Red Dragon'* patterns, both created around 1730, exemplify this Saxon creativity.[100] The Red Dragon pattern, particularly admired at various points in Meissen's history, was initially reserved for the royal court.[101] Although the design has evolved and simplified over the past three centuries, it has experienced renewed popularity in the early twenty-first century and is available in several additional colour variations. The pattern's relative obscurity in the second half of the 20th century may partly be linked to its association with the Nazi period; Adolf Hitler, for example, owned Meissen tableware with the Red Dragon pattern at his Adlershorst complex.[102] The origin of the dragon motif itself remains unclear. One account suggests it arrived in Europe from Japan around 1700, while another posits a purely German origin.[103] Like Japanese dragons, it features three claws, unlike the four or five claws typically found on Chinese dragons.[104]

Adam Friedrich von Löwenfinck represents another strand of artistic innovation at Meissen. At the age of 13, he became a student in Höroldt's workshop and worked as a painter from 1734 to 1736. Although his time at the manufactory was brief, he was one of its most original and versatile painters. Löwenfinck developed a distinctive style inspired by Japanese (Kakiemon) decorations, which he further expanded with his own imaginative forms and colours. His mythological animals, flying dogs, men on horses and camels, birds and flowers, and imagined Japanese scenes were primarily painted on tableware and decorative vessels. In modern adaptations, these motifs have also been applied to decorative objects such as pillows. Löwenfinck's younger brothers, Carl Heinrich and Christian Wilhelm, also worked in Meissen but did not achieve the same level of excellence.

The 'Indian flowers' motif, which extends beyond purely floral designs and is not of Indian origin, is likewise thought to have been inspired by the Kakiemon style. Most Asian porcelain was transported to Europe via the Dutch East Indies Company, leading to the misnomer 'Indian' for Chinese or Japanese porcelain and its decoration. In the 1730s, European flowers were introduced as inspiration for tableware decoration, leading to the creation of the 'German flowers' décor. The primary source of inspiration appears to have been Johann Wilhelm Weinmann's botanical print book *Phytanthoza iconographia*.[105] From 1745 onward, more naturalistic flowers were painted, and birds, insects, caterpillars, and spiders were added to these naturalistic decors.[106] As previously mentioned, the bourgeoisie greatly favoured the naturalistic style.

In addition to flower decorations, other East Asian motifs were gradually replaced by more European ones, often copied from or inspired by earlier copperplate engravings depicting mountain landscapes, river scenes, couples in parks, equestrian battles, etc. This shift—from East Asian-inspired decoration to naturalistic and Rococo motifs—reflects a broader reorientation of Meissen painting toward European artistic traditions. This development continued into the 1740s, by which time chinoiseries had largely fallen out of fashion. After 1740, painting also embraced the Rococo style, with the colours becoming lighter and more matte.[107]

While Augustus III decreased his orders, demand from European feudal rulers and aristocracy—particularly von Brühl and Sułkowski—steadily increased. Their interest lay less in commercial products than in bespoke creations, as displaying this 'White Gold' functioned as a marker of status and wealth. For instance, Count Heinrich von Brühl possessed one of the world's largest Meissen collections; by 1753, his palace housed some 3,000 figurines and vases.[108] Augustus III granted him the privilege of receiving these items without payment, recognizing that as Prime Minister, von Brühl entertained numerous guests and needed to showcase wealth befitting the Saxon state.[109] Other prominent clients included Count von Friesen, Cardinal Albani, Danish King Christian VI, and Count von Hennicke. Meissen creations were frequently commissioned as diplomatic gifts for other royal houses or influential figures. In 1749, for example, the Saxon Ambassador in Paris advised von Brühl to present porcelain gifts to Madame de Pompadour to leverage her influence at the Court of Louis XV.[110] These gifts served not only diplomatic purposes but also sought to persuade these royal houses to place orders with the Meissen manufactory rather than its competitors. A particularly significant example is the Russian royal court, especially under Empress Elizaveta Petrovna (r. 1741–1762), whose patronage further reinforced Meissen's international prestige.

During the 1730s and 1750s, Saxony and Russia maintained a close political and military alliance. The support of Russia, coupled with the Saxon Elector's conversion to Catholicism, contributed to his election as King of Poland and to his emergence as a leading political figure in Europe. As a token of this alliance, the Meissen manufactory sent numerous porcelain gifts to the Russian court. For instance, in 1745, Empress Elizaveta Petrovna received a 26-person table service, comprising over 400 pieces, including 190 figurines, and 90 flower vases, to celebrate the wedding of her nephew Karl Peter (the future Tsar Peter III) to Princess Sophie Auguste Friederike of Anhalt-Zerbst (the future Catherine the Great). This St. Andrew Service,[111] named after the cross of the Order of St. Andrew the First-Called, was likely the largest gift ever produced by the Meissen manufactory and the first of its kind delivered to Russia.[112]

Established in 1698 by Tsar Peter I, the Order of St. Andrew was the highest order of merit in the Russian Empire, reflecting the tradition according to which the Apostle Andrew travelled to the region of modern-day Russia in the first century AD. The service, based on the form of the Gotzkowsky relief, was further adorned with the Russian double eagle, an image of St. George, and so-called 'German flowers' (naturally rendered floral motifs). The candlesticks bear a striking resemblance to those of the Swan Service.

Each year on 30 November, the service was used at the annual banquet of the Order of St. Andrew in the Winter Palace in Saint Petersburg. To accommodate this event, the service was expanded, with many items produced at the Imperial Porcelain Factory in St. Petersburg.[113] Beyond the Empress herself, members of her government and close associates also received such gifts from the Saxon court, including table services for General Field Marshal von Münnich[114] and Grand Chancellor Bestushev.

In addition to receiving gifts, Empress Elizaveta Petrovna commissioned numerous items from Meissen. She acquired substantial quantities of tableware[115] and demonstrated a particular interest in fine art, notably the allegories of the four continents, the five senses, and the four seasons. In 1750, Johann Joachim Kändler was commissioned to create a figurine of Elizaveta Petrovna. However, both the commissioner and the intended purpose of the piece remain unclear. Since Kändler had never met Elizaveta in person, he relied on a copy of a painting by Georg Christoph Grooth to create her likeness. The figurine depicts the Empress on horseback, guided by an *arapchonok* (a young African page in Russian court service). The original painting, which served as Kändler's model, is still on display at the Tretyakov Gallery in Moscow. Grooth, a German painter who moved to Russia in 1741, was appointed Court Painter by Elizaveta two years later. In the figurine, the Empress wears the uniform of the Preobrazhensky Regiment, one of the oldest elite regiments of the Imperial Russian Army, founded by Peter the Great. She also wears the star of the Polish Order of the White Eagle on a blue ribbon over her left shoulder. This distinction, established by Augustus the Strong as King of Poland in 1705, has since been bestowed upon distinguished Poles and high-ranking foreign officials. The insignia of the Order of St. Andrew the First-Called is visible on her chest.

As interest in the Japanese Palace waned and the Rococo style gained prominence in Meissen, the manufactory shifted from producing large animal figures to smaller-scale works and more varied figurative compositions. The five modellers of the manufactory—Kändler, Eberlein, Meyer, Ehder, and Reinicke—created a wide range of such pieces, many of which are now considered among the best known and remain highly sought after. The following pages provide an overview of this diverse production, including animals, crinoline groups, saints and other religious figures, mythological and allegorical compositions, theatrical pieces, satirical figures, and representations of national types and professions.

In 1697, Augustus the Strong, ruler of the predominantly Protestant Saxony, converted to Roman Catholicism to secure his election as King of Poland-Lithuania. His son, Augustus III, followed suit in 1712, a decision that facilitated his marriage to the daughter of Habsburg Emperor Joseph I and strengthened his claim to the Polish throne. This reflects the significant role of religion in the political and social structures of the time—an importance that is also evident in 18th-century artistic production, including Meissen porcelain figurines.[116]

The first religious figurine, a *Mater Dolorosa*, appeared as early as 1719. More significant, however, are the various series of the twelve apostles, many of which were reworkings of earlier designs.[117] Primarily modelled by Kändler, with contributions from Kirchner and Eberlein, these figures were likely inspired by the marble statues by Pierre-Étienne Monnot in the Basilica of St John Lateran in Rome. Owing to the technical limitations of porcelain, however, the Meissen artists adapted the compositions, simplifying the voluminous drapery of the originals into more compact and structurally stable compositions.[118]

These series were produced in various sizes, with some examples exceeding one metre in height, though most range between 35 and 50 cm. Religious production at Meissen, however, extended well beyond apostolic figures. With Eberlein's assistance, Kändler also created busts of saints, popes, bishops, and martyrs, as well as calvaries, pietàs, and representations of the *Maria Immaculata*. A notable example is the *Maria de Victoria*, commissioned in 1737 by Maria Josepha, the devout wife of Augustus III and daughter of Emperor Joseph I. This composition depicts the Virgin Mary holding the Christ Child, standing atop a globe and subduing a dragon —a motif traditionally associated with the triumph over evil. In this version, the Child pierces the dragon with a lance; in later variants, he instead holds a cross.

Orders based on religious themes frequently combined figurines of apostles and saints with liturgical objects intended for ecclesiastical display. In 1735, for instance, Augustus III commissioned a large ensemble—known as the 'Roman Order'—as a gift for Cardinal Albani, papal nuncio in Dresden and a relative of Pope Clement XI. The commission may have served as a gesture of gratitude for Albani's support of Augustus's Polish kingship. The set, now preserved in the Cathedral of Urbino,[119] included figures of Saints Peter and Paul alongside a wide array of liturgical objects, such as a crucifix, candlesticks, chalice, holy water vessel, and monstrance.[120] In the following years, similar ensembles of apostolic figures and religious objects were produced for prominent Catholic patrons, including Wilhelmine Amalia, Empress Maria Theresa, and Empress Catherine of Russia.[121] The last major commission of this kind appears to have been the so-called '*Big Court Order*,' consisting of a series of saints and a complete altar, ordered by Pope Clement XIV in 1772 and executed in the later phase of Kändler's career.

Kändler's naturalistic approach to modelling animals, discussed earlier, is also evident in his smaller-scale animal figures. Among these, the pug occupies a particularly prominent position. Numerous compositions depict either pugs alone or figures accompanied by them. For instance, surviving examples include scenes of Freemasons seated at a globe, a Freemason attempting to kiss a woman at a table while a pug observes, as well as standalone figures of a Freemason in ceremonial dress and a woman holding a pug.[122] These pieces have been linked to the Order of the Pug, a society modelled after the Freemasons.

Following the papal condemnation of Freemasonry by Pope Clement XII in April 1738, a group of German Catholics, reportedly led by Clemens Augustus of Bavaria, established a parallel society, likely in response to the restrictions imposed by the decree.[123] This organisation adopted structures and rituals similar to those of the Freemasons while remaining formally distinct. It has been suggested that the Order of the Pug may have functioned, at least in part, as a parody of Freemasonry. At the same time, it likely fulfilled a social role, offering members of the aristocracy an alternative setting in which to replicate the rituals and ceremonial culture of the lodge.[124] The pug, widely regarded at the time as a symbol of fidelity and devotion, was adopted as the emblem of the order. It played a central role in initiation rituals, during which members were reportedly required to imitate the animal's behaviour. Unlike Freemasonry, however, the Order of the Pug admitted women and granted them equal status, suggesting that it may have functioned as a more socially inclusive—and possibly less formal—adaptation of Masonic practice.

Although the Order was officially banned in 1748, its subsequent activities remain unclear, and it may have continued to exist clandestinely for some time. It is important to note, however, that not all pug figurines can be directly associated with this context. The animal was highly fashionable among the European aristocracy more generally. Augustus the Strong, for example, is said to have presented a porcelain pug to his mistress, Countess Cosel, as a token of affection, and Kändler produced small-scale pug figures as early as 1734, prior to the establishment of the Order.

A large number of figurines and groups depicting court life were produced, frequently drawing inspiration from the paintings of Watteau, particularly in their emphasis on elegant leisure and courtly interaction.[125] Among the most notable are the so-called crinoline groups, primarily produced between 1740 and 1745. Another popular theme related to court life reflects the aristocratic fascination with pastoral simplicity, often expressed through idealised depictions of shepherd life. This trend in the early 18th century resulted in distinctive figurines of shepherds adorned in luxurious clothing. Figurines of 18th-century royalty were also created, including Augustus the Strong, Augustus III, Queen Maria Josepha, and selected Holy Roman Emperors.

Kändler produced a vast array of figures representing common professions in their professional attire, complete with relevant attributes. These included figures of beggars, farmers, winegrowers, housekeepers, wood splitters, tinkers, cooks, tailors, smiths, shoemakers, and various types of soldiers.[126] While most of these figurines were initially conceived as individual pieces, entire series were developed from the mid-1740s onward, possibly for commercial reasons, as collectors who acquired one figurine would likely be inclined to purchase the rest.[127]

One of the first series, the '*Cris de Paris,*' created around 1744-47, consisted of seven figurines, each measuring 18-19 cm in height. This series reflects the growing interest in urban street life and the representation of lower social classes in European visual culture. Meissen's archives indicate that Reinicke modelled the '*map vendor*' and the '*baker's boy,*' and it is presumed that he also created the other five.[128] These figurines were based on copper engravings by French Count Anne Claude Philippe de Caylus (published as '*Etudes prises dans le bas Peuple ou les Cris de Paris*'), which were themselves based on red chalk drawings by sculptor-architect Edme Bouchardon.[129]

In subsequent years, several other series were produced, including the Monkey Orchestra, Gallant Orchestra, Gardener Children, Paris Pedlars, and Cupids. A second '*Cris de Paris*' series, comprising 36 figures of approximately 14 cm, was initiated under Johann Joachim Kändler in 1753–54, with significant contributions from Peter Reinicke, particularly in the adaptation of French print sources.[130] In 1754, Reinicke created the *Cris de Londres*, based on a series of engravings by Pierce Tempest after Marcellus Laroon.

Another noteworthy series is Kändler's set of eight miners, created in 1750. Mining was a crucial economic sector in Saxony, and its workers had been depicted in paintings and on coins since the mid-16th century.[131] Prior to Kändler's series, the Meissen manufactory had already produced several mining-related figurines, including a Bergmannsleuchter figurine in Böttger stoneware in 1719 and a series of seven miners, most likely created by Georg Fritsche between 1725 and 1731.[132] Kändler drew visible inspiration from Christoph Weigel's engravings for seven of his eight miner figurines. Weigel's engravings were based on the miner's habit (traditional dress) of Plauen, where the clothing and attributes of each specific profession within the mining industry were regulated. For instance, workers and officials wore distinct, regulated forms of dress that reflected their rank and role within the mining hierarchy.[133] The miner's habit is still worn during processions in Saxony's old mining regions. The only figurine not based on Weigel's drawings is the triangle player, for which Kändler may have drawn inspiration from Fritsche's miners' series, which included a similar figure.[134]

Drawing upon their close familiarity with aristocratic life, Kändler and his colleagues produced satirical figurines that playfully engaged with the distinctive traits of the upper classes through caricature. A prime example is the celebrated Monkey Orchestra, initially conceived by Kändler in 1753, comprising 19 monkey figures and a music stand. The popularity of the group and sustained demand led to the deterioration of the original moulds. Consequently, Kändler, in collaboration with Reinicke, remodelled the group in 1765–66, adding two further figures: a violinist and a bagpiper. The male figures are depicted playing instruments, while the female figures appear as singers. This ensemble remains one of the most widely recognised figurine groups produced at the Meissen manufactory. Its widespread appeal prompted numerous other manufactories, including Fürstenberg, Vienna, Chelsea, Dresden, Unterweissbach, and Pößneck, to create similar monkey orchestras, some of which closely imitated the original design.[135]

The origin of the Monkey Orchestra is subject to various interpretations. According to one account, Kändler attended a dinner hosted by the Elector, where the reportedly discordant performance of the von Brühl orchestra inspired the composition as a satire of courtly musical culture.[136] Another version suggests that Kändler drew inspiration from a story in Gottlieb Wilhelm Rabener's 1745 publication, *'Neue Beyträge zum Vergnügen des Verstandes und Witzes.'* In a manner reminiscent of an Aesopian fable, the story recounts how a group of monkeys, trained and dressed as humans, reverted to their primal behaviour when presented with apples and nuts.[137]

Monkeys had appeared in European courtly culture since at least the late medieval period and were frequently satirized in literature in subsequent centuries.[138] Artists such as Antoine Coypel,

Chardin, and Watteau also incorporated the motif of monkeys imitating humans into their works.[139] Kändler was influenced by the numerous contemporary drawings and paintings depicting apes imitating human behaviour. Five figures appear to be modelled after Jean-Baptiste Guélard's copper engravings entitled *'Singeries ou différentes actions de la vie humaine représentées par des Singes'* (1741-42), which were based on drawings by Christophe Huet from 1739.[140] Two additional figures bear a striking resemblance to paintings by Huet.[141] In this context, such compositions not only entertained but also reflect a broader tradition of *'singerie,'* in which animal figures were used to comment on human behaviour and social conventions.

In 2006, to commemorate the 300th birthday of Kändler, often regarded as the *'father of European porcelain art,'* Silke Ebermann created a 22nd monkey.[142] This tambourine player, modelled after a copper engraving by Jean-Baptiste Guélard, was limited to 300 copies, with the moulds reportedly destroyed to prevent further reproduction.

One of the most notable satirical compositions from Kändler's early period at the Meissen manufactory is the 43 cm tall figure commonly known as the *'Tailor on a He-Goat'* (1737). It depicts a tailor, elegantly dressed and equipped with the tools of his trade, seated atop a goat. The spectacles worn by both figures may allude to figurative short-sightedness, reinforcing the work's satirical character. The composition has been associated with a number of anecdotal accounts involving the tailor of Count von Brühl, who is said to have sought admission to a royal dinner. In these narratives, the figure functions as a humorous commentary on social ambition and the perceived transgression of established hierarchies. Regardless of its precise origin, the model became widely collected and was reproduced by several European manufactories, including Ludwigsburg, Höchst, Derby, and Staffordshire. In later years, smaller versions were produced, and Eberlein created a companion piece representing the tailor's wife.

Closely related to this satirical approach are the figurines of the two main jesters at the Saxon Court, created by Kändler in the late 1730s and early 1740s. Jesters were highly popular at the time and often enjoyed considerable prestige, gaining recognition not only as entertainers but also as participants in courtly life. The magician and illusionist Joseph Fröhlich, known for his keen sense of humour, was one of the most prominent jesters of 18th-century Saxony. In 1733, Kändler modelled a small figurine of Fröhlich, likely based on a 1729 copper engraving by Christian Friedrich Boetius.[143] The figurine depicts him in bloomers, a short jacket, suspenders, a ruff, and a pointed hat. Although likely Kändler's first small porcelain figurine, it was remodelled several times in the following decades, including a version with a nodding head.[144] The melancholic *'Postmaster'* Schmiedel was another prominent jester. His yellow costume resembled that of a contemporary postmaster. Schmiedel was known for his convincing imitation of a phobia of mice, which Fröhlich frequently incorporated into his performances by pulling the creatures from his friend's pockets or mouth. Consequently, mice became a typical attribute for these figurines. In 1739, Augustus III commissioned Kändler to create a life-size bust of the *'Postmaster,'* intended to stand in the Japanese Palace alongside a bust of Fröhlich modelled by Kirchner around 1730. The resulting satirical portrait reflects both the melancholic character of the jester and the witty aspects of his life and work. A number of smaller compositions were produced, often featuring Fröhlich, such as the popular group depicting Fröhlich holding a mousetrap, which was remodelled numerous times. Another example is the *'Schlittengruppe,'* where Fröhlich is seen attempting to kiss a lady on a sleigh, unaware that the figure is in fact Schmiedel in disguise.

The Commedia dell'arte, popular throughout Europe, had already served as a source of inspiration for figurines and tableware decoration during the manufactory's early years. This trend continued, especially given Augustus III's fondness for Italian art. In 1737, the ruler even established a *'Comici italiani,'* employing Italian actors at his court for nearly two decades. Giovanna Farussi, mother of the famed Giacomo Casanova, was one of the theatre's most renowned performers. Under the direction of master modeller Johann Joachim Kändler, alongside collaborators such as Peter Reinicke, a series of porcelain figures depicting iconic stock characters—Harlequin, Columbine, Pantalone, and others—was produced with remarkable vitality and theatrical expressiveness. These figures translated the exaggerated gestures, masked identities, and improvisational spirit of *commedia dell'arte* into three-dimensional form, often capturing moments of flirtation, satire, and social parody. Characterized by dynamic movement, intricate costume detailing, and a keen sense of humour, these works exemplify Meissen's ability to merge sculptural innovation with contemporary cultural trends. The commedia figures not only served as decorative objects for aristocratic interiors but also functioned as subtle reflections of courtly society, mirroring its hierarchies, follies, and fascination with performance.

During the 18th century, a widespread fascination with distant regions and their inhabitants inspired Meissen modellers to create figurines representing figures from East Asia. These ranged from soldiers and merchants to sultans, all adorned in their national costumes. Numerous examples exist of Chinese, Persians, Turks, Malabars, and others, some even depicted seated on elephants or other animals. Given that the modellers at the Meissen manufactory had limited direct exposure to these regions, their understanding of these national costumes was primarily derived from paintings and drawings. For figurines representing people from the Balkans and the Middle East, Kändler and Reinicke appear to have drawn inspiration from the 1714 book, *Recueil de cent estampes représentant différentes nations du Levant*, which featured copper engravings based on drawings by Jean-Baptiste Van Mour. In many instances, the Meissen modellers often closely followed the poses found in these engravings.

THE SEVEN YEARS'
WAR: 1756–1763

The Third Silesian War between Austria and Prussia (1756-1763) formed part of the larger Seven Years' War, which involved most of the major European powers. Frederick II of Prussia invaded Saxony to establish a strategically advantageous base for attacking Austria, which had allied with France and Russia. Following several months of military engagement, the Saxon army surrendered. For the next seven years, Meissen and Saxony were occupied by the Prussians and repeatedly invaded by the Austrians, further destabilising the region. The Treaty of Hubertusburg in 1763 brought an end to the Seven Years' War, but also marked a significant decline in Saxony's political and economic position. The death of Augustus III half a year later led to the end of the Saxon-Polish personal union.

The war had severe consequences for the Meissen manufactory, posing a serious threat to its continued operation. It was closed in November 1756, but reopened five months later. No technical advancements occurred during these years of conflict, and the market demand for luxury porcelain was severely limited. The manufactory's entire warehouse stock was confiscated, and increasing financial pressures were imposed by the Prussian occupiers under threat of relocating the entire production to Berlin. As in the Second Silesian War, the arcanists (including Höroldt) fled to Frankfurt-am-Main, only to return seven years later. As Kändler did not possess complete knowledge of the Arcanum, he was permitted to remain at Meissen, where he cooperated with Frederick

II, who amassed a substantial collection of Meissen porcelain. Despite accusations of collaboration levelled against Kändler by some of his adversaries, he played a crucial role in managing the manufactory and safeguarding the interests of the employees who remained. Frederick II placed substantial orders with the manufactory, which may even have increased its staff during these war years.[145] Taken together, these conditions fundamentally altered the manufactory's production priorities, shifting its output from courtly display objects toward more pragmatic and externally commissioned works.

The manufactory's future was further jeopardised by the departure of talented artists seeking better opportunities due to decreasing salaries. The Royal Prussian Porcelain Manufactory in Berlin sought to recruit experienced personnel. In 1761, Friedrich Elias Meyer relocated to Berlin and became the manufactory's most renowned modeller. While Kändler declined a similar offer from the Prussian King, by the end of 1761, only Kändler and Reinicke remained of the five modellers, leading to the recruitment of Carl Christoph Punct to fill the void. Punct's work consists primarily of pastoral groups.[146]

While creativity persisted at the manufactory, the loss of most archives from that era complicates a full assessment of its output. New commissions appear to have come primarily from Frederick II, who frequently commissioned table services intended as diplomatic gifts.[147] The Vestunen Service, created for Frederick II, may represent one of the earliest Meissen services influenced by emerging Neoclassical taste, a trend already popular in France and England.[148] In terms of sculptural art, Kändler created a series of *Seasons* and remodelled the Monkey Orchestra during the later 1760s, adding two additional figures.

Despite these disruptions, the manufactory demonstrated a remarkable capacity for adaptation, ensuring its survival in a period of profound political and economic instability.

FRENCH INFLUENCES AND THE START OF NEOCLASSICISM: 1763–1774

The years following the Seven Years' War presented significant challenges, compelling the manufactory to adapt to new conditions. Above all, Meissen had effectively lost its earlier dominance and some of its prestige. Sèvres and Wedgwood had risen to prominence in the porcelain industry through technical and artistic innovation, while competition from other manufactories intensified. Many manufactories reproduced Meissen's designs, and some even flourished as a result of employing former Meissen artisans. Chinese porcelain also remained a significant competitor, particularly in the production of customised commissions, although this was an expensive process, particularly given the lengthy production and transport times to Europe.

The porcelain industry became increasingly global in scope, with production and trade extending across Europe and Asia, prompting the Meissen manufactory to respond to increasingly diverse market demands. For instance, between 1747 and 1797, six different models of so-called *'Turkish'* washing services (pitcher and washbowl sets) were created.[149] These items were intended not only for customers in the Ottoman Empire, an important market for European porcelain, but also for European clients. 'Alla Turca,' a common Baroque term for anything in an Ottoman or broadly Middle Eastern style (though now primarily used in music history),[150] reflected a wave of Turkish fashion that swept across Europe after the Ottoman sieges of Vienna in 1529 and 1683, inspiring many Europeans to adopt 'Turkish' styles in dress and home decoration.[151]

However, European royal courts and aristocrats increasingly diversified their patronage beyond Meissen, especially as the import and transit of Saxon porcelain had been forbidden in some places, and supported porcelain production within their own countries. Simultaneously, porcelain gained popularity among the rising bourgeoisie, who, more attuned to current fashions, looked to France as a leading influence in European artistic taste. The Meissen manufactory no longer aligned with prevailing artistic preferences and could not solely rely on its past reputation and the fading popularity of Baroque and Rococo styles. Recognizing the need for revitalization to regain prominence and economic sustainability, the manufactory initiated a series of technological and artistic reforms. Under the direction of Carl von Nimptsch, this transformation involved product diversification, the recruitment of women (primarily wives and daughters of manufactory workers), and the use of auctions to generate immediate revenue. This shift also reflects a broader transition from courtly patronage to a more diversified, market-oriented production.

To identify potential technical improvements, Meissen sent a number of its employees to study the comparative advantages of competitor porcelain producers in Germany, France, and the Netherlands. This practice may be understood as a form of commercial espionage, mirroring the practices that competitors had previously employed against Meissen.[152] Upon their return, these employees facilitated several advancements, including the development of a form of biscuit (unglazed porcelain), the introduction of new paints and enamels, and the construction of new kilns that reduced cracking. More significantly, they were tasked with studying the styles and techniques utilized by the new manufactories to align with artistic market demands. Many returned with a variety of samples and model forms. For instance, Carl Friedrich Wiedene and Christian Gotthelf Grossmann, two painters from Meissen, relocated to Sèvres in 1764 and returned less than two years later with significant experience.[153]

A related objective was to entice artists who had departed Meissen during the Seven Years' War to return. Johann Friedrich and Christian Gottlob Lücke, for example, returned from Frankenthal to Meissen in 1764, as did Christian Gottlieb Berger, who had spent five years in Sèvres, in 1766.[154] Reflecting France's cultural dominance in Europe, the Meissen leadership also sought to attract a French artist. While sculptor François-Nicolas Delaistre initially agreed to move to Meissen, he later reconsidered. Instead, French sculptor Michel Victor Acier (1736-1799), the great-grandfather of Pyotr Ilyich Tchaikovsky, moved to Saxony in the fall of 1764.

In 1764, an art school was established at the manufactory to train new students, addressing the loss of artists during the Seven Years' War. Led by Christian Wilhelm Ernst Dietrich, a professor at the Dresden Art Academy (to which the new art school was subordinated), the school, rather than fostering creativity, seemed to promote Dietrich's preference for 17th-century Dutch painters such as Rembrandt, Ostade, and Teniers. Applicants aged 14 to 16 were taught drawing, painting, and modelling skills by manufactory staff for one to two years. Following a further apprenticeship of five to six years, they could become painters or modellers in the manufactory. While this provided thorough training in technical skills, it emphasized reproducing existing artworks over creating original pieces. Six years after his appointment, Dietrich was relieved of his duties due to widespread dissatisfaction with his approach, which had failed to produce positive artistic developments. In painting, the manufactory shifted away from the gravitas of Watteau and Lancret, focusing instead on landscapes and portraits, particularly the lighter pastoral scenes of Boucher.

The arrival of the newly recruited Victor Acier, who was placed on an equal footing with the 30-year-older Kändler, led to the latter's loss of his leading role as the manufactory's main modeller, creating a strained competitive relationship. The core of this problem was not only a matter of clashing personalities but, more importantly, a difference in artistic vision. The two modellers demonstrably influenced one another, and there was no abrupt change in style. Many works from this era display an distinctive combination of styles, such as a Rococo figurine on a Neoclassical pedestal, or the use of Rococo body forms with antique-looking hair and clothing. Gradually, Neoclassical influences grew: putti and children became more slender, figurines followed the principles of triangular composition and contrapposto, and pedestals adopted the Louis XVI style. In line with emerging Neoclassical tendencies, which became increasingly influential across Europe from the 1770s onward, the focus shifted to antique-mythological and allegorical creations. While this gradual change in style is evident in Acier's works, Kändler appears to have resisted these trends. French artistic models thus played a decisive role in reshaping Meissen's visual language during this period.

Kändler, who began his career as a Baroque sculptor and successfully transitioned to Rococo, wished to remain faithful to these styles. Less inclined to adapt to the new artistic trends and market demands, he gradually became less central to the manufactory's evolving direction. However, this does not mean that Kändler became obsolete or that his creativity and imagination were extinguished. He remained in charge of orders from the Saxon Elector and other major clients who shared his passion, without being forced to succumb to Neoclassicism. Some of Kändler's most famous works were created during this time. Kändler's role finally diminished when Prince Xaver began placing his orders with Acier, who was more adept in the emerging French style.

In contrast to Kändler, Acier embraced the early French Neoclassical style in porcelain, a trend pioneered by Étienne Maurice Falconet at the Sèvres manufactory. Acier's responsibility for smaller orders from the bourgeoisie and Prince Xaver allowed him to stay abreast of contemporary trends. When he arrived in Meissen in 1764, Acier lacked specific experience in porcelain but possessed extensive knowledge of French design. He found crucial support in Johann Carl Schönheit, who had repaired models for Kändler for two decades and subsequently became Acier's primary assistant. Their collaboration proved fruitful: Schönheit instructed Acier in the technical aspects of porcelain, while Acier shared his artistic insights with Schönheit.[155] This exchange contributed to Schönheit becoming a leading sculptor at the manufactory following Acier's retirement. Acier also relied more on sketches and drawings from other artists.[156] Despite these differences, he contributed to aligning the Meissen manufactory with evolving trends and market demands. Although his tenure at the manufactory lasted only 14 years, compared to Kändler's 44, Acier's output was substantial, and his contribution to Meissen's artistic development was substantial. Many of his creations reflect civic and middle-class moral themes, such as childhood and family life.

One of Acier and Schönheit's most renowned collaborations, *The Good Mother*, depicts a woman in a Louis XVI-style armchair with three children, all dressed in the height of contemporary Parisian aristocratic fashion. The theme of the good mother was popular during the Neoclassical era. It drew inspiration from Cornelia, a 2nd-century BC figure.[157] After being widowed, she devoted herself to her children's education, leading to their success in the Roman Empire. Due to their close collaboration, distinguishing Acier's and Schönheit's individual styles is often challenging. A related example can be seen in *The Good Father*, created ten years later, which is often misattributed to Acier, although Schönheit was its creator.[158] Unlike the elegantly dressed *good mother*, this father is depicted in casual attire. Traditionally viewed as the strict head of the family, he is portrayed informally, with children crawling over him.[159]

Jean Troy, another French artist, worked at Meissen for nearly two years (September 1768 – May 1770). Intended to be the manufactory's third modeller, he was dismissed for alleged lack of diligence.[160] During his brief tenure, he created at least 14 models,[161] though the moulds for most are now lost. Among these figurines are the King Charles spaniels *Inès* and *Mimi,* the beloved pets of Madame de Pompadour, mistress of French King Louis XV. These models were created in 1769-1770, based on drawings by Christophe Huet.[162] Madame de Pompadour, a known collector of Meissen porcelain, is also said to have been among the first owners of the Meissen monkey band collection.

In Russia, porcelain gained prominence in the late 18th century, becoming essential in wealthy households. Catherine the Great was its most important patron in the second half of the century.[163] She commissioned porcelain not only for her own use but also as gifts for prominent political and military figures, such as Count Orlov and Count Rumyantsev.[164] Like many European royals of her time, the Russian Empress was passionate about hunting, including the associated banquets and festivities. In 1766, she ordered a hunting-themed table service for her Tsarskoe Selo hunting lodge. Comprising approximately 1,000 pieces, it was the second-largest service of the 18th century, after Count von Brühl's Swan Service. While archival evidence remains inconclusive, Victor Acier is the likely modeller of this service. Dozens of painters were employed to execute the detailed hunting scenes on the vessels. The Imperial Russian Manufactory continued to expand this service in subsequent years.[165]

In 1770, Kändler created an equestrian figurine of Catherine the Great. Its creation and attributes share similarities with the figurine of Elizaveta Petrovna, suggesting it was based on the famous 1762 painting *'Trip to Peterhof'* by Virgilius Eriksen, the Danish imperial court painter in St. Petersburg. Like Elizaveta's figurine, Catherine the Great is depicted wearing the uniform of the Preobrazhensky Regiment.

Probably the most impressive commission during the late 18th century was the *'Great Russian Order'* of Catherine the Great. In 1772, she commissioned a series of 40 figural groups[166] intended to glorify her achievements through depictions of mythological deities and allegorical representations of the Empress and her Empire. This project marked the first major collaboration between Kändler and Acier. While Kändler created the drawings for all the groups, he only modelled the 19 largest works, leaving the 21 smaller ones to his colleague. Kändler skilfully combined his knowledge of mythology with contemporary Russian political events, particularly in the military sphere. These works were originally placed in Oranienbaum, but many were vandalized or stolen in 1917.

Another notable composition is a figurine of a greyhound created by Kändler in 1766, based on a drawing from Moscow. It is said to depict Lisetta, Catherine the Great's favourite dog, but the physiology does not match that of a female dog.

Together, these developments illustrate how Meissen navigated a shifting artistic and economic landscape, adapting to new international influences while maintaining elements of its established identity.

NEOCLASSICISM AND THE MARCOLINI ERA: 1774 – 1814

In the following decades, the manufactory faced an increasingly precarious financial situation. Orders and sales declined despite the continued high quality of its production. Imitations and counterfeit wares were circulating, and competition from other manufactories, especially Sèvres, Berlin, and Vienna, intensified. The production of fine porcelain became less dependent on royal patronage and more reliant on commercial and organisational expertise.[167] Cheaper ceramics, such as faïence, also competed with porcelain, as the bourgeoisie lacked the financial means of the aristocracy. English porcelain and tableware entered European markets in large quantities during the 1780s, and Meissen even began imitating these goods. The proliferation of porcelain manufactories throughout Europe diminished porcelain's exclusivity, and it became less frequently used as a royal diplomatic gift from the late 18th century onwards. Russia remained the most important market during the last decades of the 18th century, with Meissen exporting as much as 40% of its production there in the 1770s.[168]

Count Camillo Marcolini (1739-1814) succeeded von Nimptsch as director in 1774, with the aim of stabilising the manufactory's finances. Marcolini focused on restoring financial sustainability, approaching the issue primarily from an economic and administrative perspective. During his tenure, there were few technological or chemical innovations, with the exception of the wider adoption of biscuit (unglazed porcelain) around 1780, a technique developed in soft paste at Vincennes in 1751. Marcolini lacked an artistic background and appears to have placed less emphasis on artistic innovation within the manufactory. The strained relationship between Kändler and Acier further complicated Marcolini's challenges. Although Marcolini implemented stricter controls, lowered salaries, and reduced staff, these measures proved insufficient, ultimately requiring financial support from the Elector. In 1799, Marcolini tendered his resignation but was persuaded by the Elector to remain in his position.

The political upheavals following the French Revolution of 1789 led to a significant decline in orders for Meissen porcelain. Russia and, for a time, the Ottoman Empire remained important exceptions. However, when Ottoman orders also declined due to continuous military setbacks against the Russian Empire, Russia became the primary remaining market for Meissen porcelain. The situation in Europe was further aggravated by the Napoleonic Wars and the imposition of high import duties and restrictions by countries seeking to protect and promote their domestic porcelain production. In July 1806, Saxony joined Napoleon's Confederation of the Rhine and was rewarded with an upgrade from an Electorate to a Kingdom. However, with Russia at war with Napoleon, the Russian court banned the import of porcelain from its adversaries, including Meissen. At the same time, cheaper French porcelain gained increasing popularity in European markets.

Adding to these challenges, the Meissen manufactory faced difficulties related to kaolin quality and outdated equipment, resulting in production losses that reportedly reached as high as 75%.[169] Consequently, overall sales of Meissen porcelain halved in 1806. By 1809, the government considered decommissioning the enterprise, as many other European porcelain manufactories had already closed. Sales continued to fall, and by 1813, the manufactory's survival was increasingly uncertain, with sales plummeting to less than one-sixth of what they had been eight years prior.[170] Hopes for a swift return to the Russian market remained unfulfilled.

In September-October 1813, Meissen found itself on the front lines between French and Prussian-Cossack forces. Although initially planning to position troops at the Albrechtsburg, the French ultimately did not do so. Following the retreat of Napoleon's forces, Russian and Prussian troops took control of the city, and the castle was repurposed as a hospital. As a result of this conflict, the manufactory was forced to close entirely, and much of its equipment was destroyed or confiscated. In 1814, Marcolini resigned from the manufactory, which survived only through subsidies, and died six months later. He was ultimately unable to restore the manufactory to the glory it had experienced under Brühl.

Despite some art critics judging the Marcolini era as one marked by artistic decline, a lack of creativity, and excessive imitation of competitors, this period possessed its own unique character and merits, which can be understood within the specific artistic and economic context.

By the start of the Marcolini period, the Louis XVI style had become dominant in Meissen, representing both the final stage of Rococo and the initial stage of neoclassicism. For example, the rocaille ornament was abandoned after 1774. Dietrich's emphasis on antique inspiration influenced both the sculptural and painted aspects of the pieces, resulting in a style referred to as *'à la Grèque'*. This style favoured straight lines and a rich repertoire of decorative motifs, including ribbons, entwined rods, pearl beading, bands, laurel wreaths, floral sprigs, torches, sickles, thyrsus rods, and meander and palmetto ornaments. The same trends extended to painting, with increased use of black and sepia tones. Garnitures often featured miniature portraits or silhouettes or imitated materials like pearl grey marble, lapis lazuli, or porphyry. The painting and decoration of tableware primarily focused on native birds, butterflies, insects, and flowers.[171]

Neoclassicism gained momentum as the demand for Rococo declined sharply, reflecting broader social and economic transformations, including the rise of a middle class, particularly after the French Revolution. A growing trend in the porcelain industry involved reproducing existing sculptural models on a reduced scale. Biscuit porcelain, resembling marble and alabaster, proved particularly well-suited for this purpose, as it allowed for a more precise rendering of the human form. Given that most new creations of the time were derived from existing models, identifying specific modellers in Meissen based on stylistic features alone is difficult, making historical archives the primary source of information.

Johann Joachim Kändler produced few new objects during the Marcolini era, as he died from a stroke in 1775 at the age of 69, after a 44-year career at the Meissen manufactory. Michel Victor Acier, who became the principal modeller at the manufactory, created some of his best works in the years following 1775. He retired in 1780 but continued to produce pieces occasionally in subsequent years.

Following Acier's retirement, the Meissen manufactory benefited from a cohort of talented and well-trained artists. While some of Kändler and Acier's assistants embraced the burgeoning Neoclassical trends, the manufactory's artistic direction shifted away from in-house artists, becoming increasingly influenced by external sources, particularly the Art Academy.[172] Unlike their predecessors, Johann Carl Schönheit, Christian Gottfried Jüchtzer, and Johann Gotlieb Matthai fostered a collaborative environment, inspiring and assisting one another.[173] They produced smaller biscuit porcelain versions of sculptures from the Dresden Art Collections, which proved popular among the Enlightenment bourgeoisie. However, this meant the modellers were primarily copying existing works, thereby entering into competition with bronze and gypsum reproductions. Innovation during this period often operated within the framework of adaptation and reinterpretation rather than entirely original invention. Furthermore, a significant number of works from the Marcolini era drew inspiration from paintings by artists such as Boucher, Chardin, Greuze, and Fragonard, as well as sculptors like Pigalle and Falconet.[174] While new creations were typically the domain of modellers, some figurines were also produced by moulders, including Christian Carl Fischer junior and Friedrich Gotthelf Schmieder.

Johann Carl Schönheit joined the manufactory at the age of fifteen, spending his first twenty years assisting Kändler and the subsequent fifteen with Acier. Although he created some original works before Acier's retirement, most date from after 1780. Notable examples include the *Jahreszeiten* (1782), based on designs by J.E. Schenau, *Die Weinlese* and *Die Weinpresse* (1785 and 1786), *Die Edle Aufschub* (1787), *Die Entschlossene Wahl* (1786), and *Liebe und Belohnung*.[175] In the years leading up to his retirement, he focused on copying statues and motifs from antiquity in biscuit porcelain.[176] Christian Gottfried Jüchtzer succeeded Schönheit, joining Acier's workshop. Examples of his work include *Three Graces*. Examples of Matthai's work include *Gladiator*.

Until the 19th century, the Russian aristocracy and bourgeoisie represented Meissen's largest market. While sales figures did not reach previous heights, special commissions continued to be produced for the Tsars. For instance, the Russian court commissioned an allegorical figurine commemorating the 1783 unification of Crimea with Russia, marking another victory of the Russian Empire against the Ottomans. This piece, a collaborative effort by Schönheit and Jüchtzer, stands as the largest biscuit porcelain group ever produced at Meissen, measuring 87 cm in height. Rather than depicting a specific historical event, the composition presents the annexation in allegorical terms, with a personification of Russia receiving or subduing a female figure representing Crimea, accompanied by symbolic figures such as Victory and Fame, and framed within a classical visual language. Another significant creation was a centrepiece comprising seven white porcelain groups created in 1779 by Acier for Nikolaj Vasilyevich Repnin. This centrepiece was gifted to the Russian Field Marshal in recognition of his crucial role in securing a peace treaty between Prussia and Austria, which contributed to stabilising Saxony. Only two groups—one depicting the *History of Saxony* and the other *Russia's Flourishing Trade*—have survived to the present day.

Following Jüchtzer's departure around 1801, Johann Daniel Schöne emerged as one of the leading modellers at the manufactory, working alongside colleagues such as Carl August Starcke senior, Carl Gotthelf Starcke junior, and Franz Andreas Weger. Schöne began his education at the Meissen academy in 1783 and, six years later, became a bosserer, primarily responsible for repairing and occasionally finalizing models by Schönheit and Jüchtzer.[177] However, in subsequent years, he also created his own models, including an *Amor am Altar,* candlesticks, and a sphinx.

Even in the late 18th century, a new stylistic influence began to emerge, deviating from the neoclassical ideal. Similar to creations at the Fürstenberg manufactory since the 1780s, and reflecting the educated middle class's literary interests, busts of political figures, famous writers, and philosophers were produced.[178] These included figures such as Cicero, Socrates, Marcolini, Russian Emperor Alexander I, Johann Friedrich Böttger, Napoleon Bonaparte, French King Louis IX, and Augustus III. Like the classicist pieces, these busts were based on existing sculptures, made of biscuit porcelain, and left unpainted. This trend away from classicism intensified in the first decade of the 19th century. Around 1790, a trend toward literary-themed porcelain emerged, with plates, cups, and vases decorated with scenes from literary works, such as Ovid's *Metamorphoses*,[179] Alexander Pope's *'Eloise to Abelard,'*[180] and John Langhorne's *'Letters between Theodosius and Constantia.'*[181]

BIEDERMEIER: 1814–1850

Although the Biedermeier period is conventionally dated from 1815 to 1848, 1814 marks an important institutional turning point for the Meissen manufactory. The period between the end of the Napoleonic Wars in 1815 and the revolutions of 1848 in Europe is known in Central Europe as the Biedermeier period. The term derives from the satirical figure '*Gottlieb Biedermaier*,' created by Ludwig Eichrodt and Adolf Kußmaul as a parody of middle-class life. In Central Europe, the period is often associated with relative political stabilization after the Napoleonic Wars and with the growing cultural importance of the middle classes. The bourgeoisie's tastes differed markedly from those of the aristocracy, prompting the manufactory to make the difficult decision in 1814 to prioritize production based on market demand over purely artistic pursuits. While this decision drew criticism from art critics and artists within the manufactory, it proved to be an effective strategy for improving the company's financial standing. The Biedermeier period is not defined by a single artistic style but rather by a pluralism of styles, including Romanticism, Neo-Gothicism, Neo-Renaissance, and Naturalism.

Although some scholars have criticized the artistic developments at the Meissen manufactory during the Biedermeier period, it was a crucial moment for its future. Meissen faced significant financial problems due to reduced sales: the Russian and Turkish markets were largely lost or severely disrupted from 1806 onward, feudal orders dwindled, and the manufactory struggled to compete on price with French porcelain.[182] By 1820, the situation was so dire that the King considered selling the manufactory, but ultimately refused, fearing it would lead to the collapse of this Saxon symbol of prosperity.[183] Unlike many competitors, the manufactory survived. This survival depended in large part on a substantial program of reforms and improvements, which coincided with increasing sales, especially after Saxony joined the German Customs Union in 1834.

During the industrial revolution of the early 19th century, many manufactories became factories, with machines taking over much of the work. Although broader trends of mechanization prompted organizational and technical adjustments at Meissen, they did not fundamentally alter its character as a manufactory in which manual labour still predominated. For this reason, it was sometimes regarded as old-fashioned or backward.[184] From a later perspective, this conservative approach may also be seen as one factor in the preservation of Meissen's artisanal identity. The Biedermeier period saw a significant shift in the demand for porcelain for several reasons. The Napoleonic Wars had caused a general economic decline in Europe, reducing the purchasing power of the nobility and bourgeoisie. However, the industrial revolution led to renewed prosperity and strengthened the middle class, who favoured a different and less expensive style.

When Carl Wilhelm von Oppel became director in 1814, the heavily subsidized manufactory still catered to a luxury market. While Meissen's competitors had also suffered economic hardship, their broader market involvement allowed for easier adaptation. To restore economic viability, von Oppel focused on cost reduction and quality improvement, emphasizing technical aspects over artistic innovation. He found support in Heinrich Gottlieb Kühn (1788-1870), head of the technical department, whose background in mining, chemistry, and law proved invaluable. This technical focus, however, did not stifle creativity. On the contrary, diverse artistic influences permeated the manufactory, resulting in numerous new designs and patterns for both fine art and household porcelain. After a few years, sales gradually increased, profitability returned, and the threat of closure subsided.

Kühn, who dedicated 56 years to the manufactory, travelled throughout Europe to study competitors' production processes. This research informed significant improvements in production, product quality, and cost reduction. In 1814, he abandoned the long-held secrecy surrounding the *Arcanum* to streamline production and encourage experimentation. He also implemented a more precise cost calculation system, invested in new machinery and more energy-efficient kilns, introduced a cheaper gilding technique that eliminated the need for post-firing polishing, sourced kaolin from a closer location to reduce transport costs, and improved the quality of the porcelain paste. Kühn continued his reforms and innovations, including the introduction of coal-fired kilns to replace more expensive wood. Social reforms were also enacted, such as the creation of a pension fund in 1840 and a worker's council in 1849. Several of these inventions and improvements deserve closer attention because of their significance. Taken together, these reforms reflect a systematic shift toward efficiency, standardization, and cost control, aligning the manufactory more closely with emerging industrial practices.

One of the most significant advancements, impacting technical, artistic, and financial aspects, concerned gilding. White porcelain with gilding became fashionable, and French manufacturers could produce it at a much lower cost than Meissen. This advantage stemmed primarily from a different type of porcelain, which, though of slightly lower quality, required firing at lower temperatures. This lower temperature requirement also allowed for a less liquid gold paint, further reducing costs.[185] Previously, Meissen's gold paint contained 40 to 60% pure gold, and after firing, the gold appeared grey-brown, necessitating manual polishing with an agate pen to achieve shine—hence the name *'polished gold.'*

Between 1815 and 1820, new gilding techniques emerged, using 50 to 75% less gold while still requiring polishing. However, these techniques were less durable and thus suitable only for surfaces, not borders or corners.[186] Often referred to as '*triangle gold*,' items decorated with this gilding bear a small red triangle next to the crossed swords trademark.[187]

In 1827, Kühn developed a new gold paint based on experiments conducted a year earlier by the French porcelain painter Desgermain.[188] This paint required only a quarter of the gold used previously, and polishing could be mechanized, yielding substantial financial benefits. A major drawback, however, was its limited durability, prompting further improvements in subsequent decades. Reportedly, this new gilding method required up to ten times less gold than the methods used two decades prior. Despite this advancement, the older, heavier gilding procedure remained in use for more valuable items when greater durability was needed.

By the second half of the 19th century, the pursuit of improved and cheaper gilding methods diminished, largely because the demand for white porcelain with gilding had almost disappeared.

To reduce costs and compete with other manufacturers, new decorating techniques were introduced. Bat-printing, already in use in France and England, was adopted at Meissen in 1815. This complex transfer-printing method involved stippling a design onto a copper plate, which was then used to transfer paint pigment onto the porcelain. This technique simplified the printing of landscapes and was especially useful for reproducing the contours of drawings with consistent shape and size, an important consideration for tableware. It also accelerated the painter's work by eliminating the need for freehand drawing, which was less precise. Initially used only for overglaze painting, a technique was developed in 1827 to apply it to underglaze painting as well.[189] Bat-printing remained in use at Meissen until the 1850s before disappearing completely.[190] However, freehand painting was still practiced in the first half of the 19th century; bat-printing was primarily used to reduce production costs for high-demand items.

Another significant innovation was the introduction of a green underglaze colour paint in 1814.[191] Unlike underglaze blue, the chromium oxide green pigment remained between the porcelain and the glaze and was not absorbed by the dried, unglazed porcelain.[192] Over the following years, approximately sixty different decoration patterns for tableware were developed, with two becoming particularly popular until 1835.[193] In 1817, Johann Samuel Arnhold developed the vine leaf pattern, which rivalled the blue onion pattern in popularity. The lancet arch design also gained considerable admiration. These technological advancements helped the manufactory reassert its position among the leading European producers.

The manufactory had been part of the King's possessions since its creation. This changed with the first Saxon constitution of 1831, which established a parliamentary monarchy. Consequently, the manufactory was placed under state ownership, with its administration directly subordinated to the Ministry of Finance and controlled by the regional parliament. This institutional change reinforced the expectation that the manufactory should operate as a financially viable enterprise rather than as a courtly prestige institution. Despite this change, the word 'Royal' remained in the manufactory's name until 1918. The elimination of the royal court's role also meant the manufactory lost its privileges, including freedom from taxes and tariffs, access to low-cost raw materials and fuel, and a monopoly within the kingdom. The parliament expected the state-owned enterprise to contribute to the state budget rather than require subsidies, which further compelled the manufactory administration to pursue economic sustainability. From 1834 onward, state contributions were no longer necessary, and profits steadily increased.

As previously noted, the Biedermeier period encompasses a pluralism of artistic styles rather than a single, unified trend. This stylistic pluralism is particularly evident in the coexistence of lingering Neoclassical forms with Romantic, Neo-Gothic, and revived Rococo tendencies. Around the time of the Napoleonic Wars, the Romantic movement gained momentum, influencing art at

Meissen. A key concept of Romanticism was nationalism, which shifted artistic focus from admiration of antiquity to a rediscovery of national history, art, and religion, particularly those of the Middle Ages and their national heroes. This led to a renewed interest in Gothic and Renaissance art, as well as a resurgence of naturalism. Although the Meissen manufactory was no longer the undisputed leader in porcelain art and, in some respects, lagged behind competitors such as Sèvres, Vienna, and Nymphenburg, it successfully re-established itself and enjoyed growing popular demand.

Neoclassicism was clearly declining, and the use of biscuit porcelain decreased significantly, although it experienced a resurgence in the 1840s.[194] The new Romantic trend emphasized depictions of people rather than deities or mythological figures. The Meissen modellers, led by Johann Daniel Schöne, continued to create figurines, busts, and relief medallions of famous artists, writers, scientists, theologians, and politicians, such as Mozart, Beethoven, Martin Luther, and King Friedrich Augustus I. These were often reproductions of bronze or stone sculptures, which meant that the modellers focused more on replication than on original creativity. This, however, does not imply a lack of talent or creative ability, as they often deviated from the original sculptures.

The number of new figurines created during this era is relatively small. One of the most famous examples produced during the Biedermeier period is the *'Chocolate Girl,'* created between 1837 and 1842, although the sculptor's identity remains unknown. The porcelain version is significant as an example of the translation of a celebrated Dresden painting into three-dimensional form and reflects the manufactory's growing engagement with well-known pictorial models. The figurine was based on the painting *'The Chocolate Girl'* by the Swiss artist Jean-Etienne Liotard, created in 1744. Augustus III later acquired the painting, which is now on display in the Old Masters Picture Gallery in Dresden. It may be the first painting to depict a Meissen object, and the Meissen Manufactory may have modelled the girl in porcelain as a gesture of appreciation. The girl's identity, however, remains unclear. One account suggests that Liotard was so captivated by the beauty of Austrian Empress Maria Theresa's maid that he immortalized her in the painting. A more romanticized version tells the story of Prince Dietriechstein, who, upon tasting the then-trendy hot chocolate in a Viennese coffee house, fell in love with the waitress, Anna Baldtauff, and married her. He is said to have commissioned the painting as a wedding gift. However, this romantic version is historically inaccurate, as the marriage occurred in 1802, 57 years after the painting was created. A third version identifies the girl as Charlotte Baldauf, the daughter of a Viennese banker.

Around 1840, a figurine of Fanny Elßler (both in biscuit and in porcelain with overglaze painting) was produced, based on Jean-Auguste Barre's bronze figurine *'Fanny Elssler dansant la cha-chucha'* from a few years prior.

From 1822 onwards, increased demand for Rococo figurines from English traders proved advantageous for the manufactory, as it required little creativity from the artists who were trained in reproducing existing designs. A similar interest arose in exports to the Russian and Ottoman Empires in the following years, leading to a kind of neo-Rococo or *'second Rococo'* style for the manufactory. In the 1840s, demand for Rococo also re-emerged from within Germany, resulting in the creation of new objects in the same style.

To diversify sales, the Meissen manufactory constantly sought new porcelain items to produce. A successful example from the two decades after 1814 is that of tobacco pipes, which at some fairs constituted up to a quarter of sales.[195] The porcelain pipe bowls were often decorated with paintings of angels, famous people, and other related themes of the era, and frequently utilized the newly invented underglaze green colour.

In 1827, the French diplomat Paul de Bourgoing received a patent for lithophanes, a new type of porcelain artwork. Lithophanes are etched artworks on a thin, translucent biscuit plaque that become more visible when backlit; thinner areas appear brighter, while thicker areas appear darker. Although similar techniques using varying thicknesses of porcelain to manipulate light and shade had been previously experimented with in China and Worcester, lithophanes quickly gained popularity throughout Europe. They were used in windows, as *Lichtschirme* in frames, and even as parts of *Lampenglocken*.[196] By 1828, the Meissen manufactory had introduced lithophanes into its production program, but initially faced challenges in finding the right porcelain paste.[197] Unlike standard porcelain, where the material's quality is paramount, lithophanes prioritize the effect of manipulating light and shade.[198] Between 1828 and 1860, some 250 different lithophane motifs were created, accounting for up to 10% of sales in the late 1830s and early 1840s.[199] Lithophanes thus exemplify the manufactory's ability to develop technically innovative products with broad middle-class appeal. Inspiration for these objects was most often drawn from paintings in the Dresden Gallery, focusing on religious scenes, city views, family and children scenes, as well as images of philosophers or European nobility.[200] The creation of these new works required a high degree of talent from the artists; for example, Habenicht produced some 130 different motifs, and Schiebell made most of the remaining ones. Although some other manufactories produced coloured lithophanes, it is unclear whether Meissen did so.[201] Around 1860, lithophanes fell out of fashion.[202]

While Johann Martin Heinrici had produced reproductions of paintings on porcelain in Meissen in the 1750s, the practice became a new type of product in the 1850s. This resurgence may have been inspired by Bavarian King Ludwig I's decision to have all the paintings in his Royal Gallery reproduced on porcelain plaques, a more durable material than canvas.[203] Meissen artists also drew upon the extensive collection of paintings in the Dresden Gallery as source material for these porcelain reproductions.

However, in the years following 1814, porcelain figurines and artworks occupied a minor position in the Meissen manufactory's output due to limited demand for luxury goods. Tableware, particularly simpler designs and decorations, constituted the bulk of sales. A rare exception is a dessert set of 134 pieces produced around 1818. Though simple in form, the porcelain was finely painted with landscapes and scenes related to the life of the Duke of Wellington,[204] who defeated Napoleon at the Battle of Waterloo in 1815. This set was a gift from Frederick Augustus III of Saxony (who had remained loyal to Napoleon) to the Duke of Wellington. Other European royal houses also sent exquisite presents, including porcelain tableware sets from Louis XVIII of France, Franz I of Austria, and Frederick William III of Prussia.

As Baroque and Rococo tableware designs gave way to simpler, more restrained styles, manufactories in Sèvres, Vienna, and Berlin gained prominence. Meissen successfully adapted to this *'new taste,'* following their lead.[205] By utilizing new techniques for gold decorations, Meissen competed with other manufactories in producing white tableware with gold borders, a style that gained popularity in the 1820s.[206]

In 1817, a second-class porcelain, decorated exclusively with underglaze painting, was introduced, followed by a third-class porcelain for pharmacy use in 1822.[207] The second-class porcelain's affordability led to its widespread popularity, but its production ceased in 1824.[208] The resurgence of underglaze decorations, which had waned under Neoclassical influences, can be attributed to their lower cost (due to less detailed painting and one less firing) and the decoration's robustness, making the tableware suitable for frequent use in bourgeois households.[209] New designs, such as vine or lancet arch motifs, were developed alongside older ones to reflect contemporary artistic trends. Georg Friedrich Kersting (1785-1847), head of the painting department, played a pivotal role in this development. Around 1820, he drew inspiration from Neo-Gothicism to create a lancet arch design, which became the second most popular décor utilizing the newly developed green underglaze paint.[210] Over the next three decades, Gothic and, to a lesser extent, Neo-Renaissance influences were evident in other tableware designs. This underglaze-painted tableware remained highly sought after until approximately 1835.[211]

Kersting also drew inspiration from naturalism, reviving floral decorations on tableware. For example, he created the 'Meissen rose' in 1820. The romantic trend is also reflected in landscape paintings, city views, and depictions of German and world literature, as well as historical events on household porcelain and vases.[212] These vessels, plates, and cups featuring paintings of people, places, or events were often used as decorative elements rather than functional tableware. The demand for floral and landscape painting increased again in the late 1830s.[213] Subsequently, tableware and vases were increasingly adorned with more elaborate paintings.

In 1831, the Meissen manufactory introduced a new tableware shape inspired by cut and polished glass crystal. This innovation, often paired with new gilding techniques, generated significant demand, reportedly accounting for nearly half of the overall sales at one point and stimulating customer interest worldwide. Carl Gotthelf Habenicht and Georg Friedrich Kersting primarily designed these models, with bas-relief decorations added over time. Although this tableware, with its glass crystal shapes and patterns, remained fashionable for the next 25 years and significantly boosted Meissen's popularity, interest in this style eventually declined, and it came to be regarded as stylistically inappropriate.[214]

In 1843, Georg Friedrich Kersting designed the service form X 17-19 as part of the 'second Rococo' movement. In porcelain, this style was widely copied throughout Europe and became known as 'Old Meissen,' essentially emulating the Rococo and Baroque styles that had initially established Meissen's reputation.

Taken together, these developments illustrate how the Meissen manufactory successfully adapted to the shifting economic and cultural conditions of the early 19th century. While no longer defined by courtly patronage or singular artistic innovation, it developed new forms of production, decoration, and distribution that aligned with the demands of a broader consumer base. In this sense, the Biedermeier period marks not a decline, but a redefinition of Meissen's identity within an increasingly modern and market-oriented context.

HISTORICISM: 1850 – 1895

The economic expansion in Europe continued throughout the second half of the 19th century, leading to an increased demand for household porcelain, particularly pieces with underglaze painting. Similar to the Biedermeier period, the historicist era was characterized by a stylistic pluralism, primarily drawing inspiration from the styles that had previously brought fame and prestige to Meissen. Historicism in this context refers to the deliberate revival and recombination of earlier artistic styles. Following his appointment as director in 1849, Kühn continued his program of technical reforms, including the introduction of filter presses, mills, and beaters, which led to increased profitability until his death in 1870.

One of the most significant developments of the mid-19th century was the relocation of the manufactory between 1863 and 1865 to a newly constructed complex in the Triebisch River valley, where it remains today. In previous decades, expansions to production capacity had been achieved through the acquisition of buildings in the immediate vicinity of the Albrechtsburg. However, this was no longer a viable option. Moreover, the Albrechtsburg was unsuitable for housing new machinery, such as steam engines, one of which even damaged the building in 1853, and stamp mills. The primary impetus for the relocation, however, came from elsewhere. In 1852, the Assembly of German History and Antiquity Researchers appealed to Saxon King Friedrich Augustus II to protect the historic Albrechtsburg, describing it as one of the most magnificent medieval buildings.[215] Discussions regarding a potential relocation intensified, and newspaper articles helped to amplify the pressure to preserve the Albrechtsburg. Simultaneously, there were concerns that the manufactory might leave Meissen, which would have had a significantly negative impact on the city, whose economy was heavily dependent on this state-owned enterprise.[216] Concurrently, negotiations took place with Belgian investors regarding the privatization of the manufactory, but these talks ultimately failed, and the Saxon state instead allocated 300,000 Thalers for the construction of the new facility.[217] Following the manufactory's departure, the Albrechtsburg underwent a complete renovation and has served as a museum since 1881.

Industrialization transformed transport and mobility, facilitating easier travel and the exchange of goods. This, in turn, spurred a greater interest in global developments, leading to the inception of the World Expositions. First held in London in 1851, these events continue to be organized every few years. Given its status under the Saxon Ministry of Finance and its role as a prominent artistic institution in Saxony, it was natural for the Meissen manufactory to participate. Over the second half of the 19th century, the manufactory exhibited at major international expositions, including London (1851, 1862), Paris (1867, 1900), Vienna (1873), and Chicago (1893). These expositions provided valuable opportunities to present Meissen's production to a global audience and explore potential new markets. For instance, at the 1851 London exhibition, the manufactory sent additional items due to unexpectedly high demand.[218] Furthermore, the events served as platforms for observing and comparing the output of rival manufactories, fostering technical and artistic innovation.

One significant consequence of the World Exhibitions was the influence of Japanese porcelain, prominently displayed in Paris in 1867 and at subsequent events. The simple forms and abstract, monochrome glazes of East Asian ceramics paved the way for aesthetic developments that would become central in the late

19th and early 20th centuries.[219] Many European porcelain producers adopted these colour-glazing and art-glazing techniques in the 1870s, but faced a significant challenge. European porcelain, due to its higher kaolin content, requires higher firing temperatures than its Asian counterpart. This meant that certain colour-glazing and art-glazing techniques, such as the coveted copper red *sang de boeuf*, were initially unattainable.[220] Consequently, many manufactories turned to soft-paste porcelain, which fires at lower temperatures but is less durable. However, the leadership at Meissen, unwilling to compromise on its commitment to exceptional quality, particularly for household porcelain where durability is paramount, pursued experimentation with artistic glazes for hard-paste porcelain. During the 1880s, Julius Heinze, the head of the laboratory, successfully developed a range of new colour glazes, including the copper red *sang de boeuf* in 1883, followed by grey, yellow, brown, and soft red variations. Despite this technological advantage, the Meissen manufactory did not consistently capitalize on its innovative glaze techniques, perhaps due to its continued focus on historically derived styles and established product lines.

An important artistic novelty was the introduction of the *pâte-sur-pâte*, or slip-painting, technique. In this technique, the artist paints with liquid porcelain slip on a coloured porcelain object, creating a relief by applying layer after layer, up to 30 in total. Once the decoration is complete, the entire object is covered with a thin layer of transparent glaze and fired. Louis Robert invented *pâte-sur-pâte* in Sèvres in the early 1850s, but the Meissen manufactory did not fully master the technique until 1878. This extremely difficult and expensive painting method was mainly used between 1880 and 1910, especially for vases and boxes. Notably, the allegorical and mythological figures of the old Meissen style once again served as the main themes for *pâte-sur-pâte* decoration.[221] A brilliant example of this technique is the jewellery box chest created by Ludwig Sturm for the 1893 World Exhibition in Chicago, which was recreated in 2016.

Despite these innovations, the focus of the modellers and painters during the historicist period remained on reproducing the Meissen heritage. There was strong demand for the '*old Meissen style*,' and the manufactory was able to profit from both old and new objects in Baroque, Rococo, and neoclassical styles. When the royal houses began patronizing the manufactory again in the 1870s, the demand for older forms and decorations increased, launching a '*third Rococo*.'[222] Bavarian King Ludwig II ordered a large number of vases, figurines, and candelabra based on models by Kändler and his colleagues; the King was also personally involved in the design of many new Rococo-style objects.[223] Tableware with the Blue Onion decoration also achieved its greatest success in the late 19th century, with more than 700 articles on offer featuring this design. In the following decades, '*ordinary blue*' became so popular—with many other manufactories counterfeiting it, including Wedgwood and Villeroy & Boch—that in 1888, the Meissen manufactory began adding the crossed swords trademark to the base of the bamboo stem in the design.

Most often, Rococo figurines were remodelled, not only because many of the original moulds were no longer usable, but also to correspond to market tastes. Ernst August Leuteritz is an important name in this respect; he reshaped existing Baroque and Rococo figurines to suit contemporary tastes, not only through modifications to form but also through changes in decoration, bases, and surface treatment. His interventions frequently included the addition of more elaborate floral ornament, heightened polychromy, and redesigned pedestals, which altered the visual balance of the original compositions. For example, earlier Kändler models were often reissued with richer surface decoration and more ornate bases, aligning them with the 19th-century preference for decorative abundance. At the same time, Leuteritz developed new forms inspired by historical models, such as his widely popular snake-handled vases, which combined historicist references with contemporary design sensibilities. His work thus illustrates how Meissen's historicism operated not as simple reproduction, but as an active process of reinterpretation. Leuteritz also developed new tableware, and both his B-form and X-form enjoyed considerable demand.

One impressive example of the Meissen manufactory's exceptional craftsmanship is the *'Fürstenzug'* or *'Procession of Princes,'* a mural located on the northern side of the Stables Courtyard of the Dresden Castle. Spanning 968 m2 (120 meters long and 10.5 meters high, though punctuated by windows), it is the largest porcelain wall painting in the world. The wall had previously been adorned with a massive fresco in 1589, which was replaced in 1873 by a sgraffito mural (a technique involving layers of plaster tinted in contrasting colours applied to a moistened surface). However, like its predecessor, this sgraffito mural by Wilhelm Walther suffered extensive damage from humidity in under 25 years. To ensure a more durable replacement, Saxon King Georg commissioned a porcelain decoration. The approximately 23,000 tiles, each measuring 20.5 by 20.5 cm, were prepared in 1905-06 and affixed to the wall. The mural depicts 35 Saxon rulers alongside 58 musicians, painters, military officers, and other figures. Only three years after installation, some tiles exhibited damage, likely due to thermal stress. Despite the near-total destruction of Dresden's city centre in February 1945, the Fürstenzug sustained only minimal damage, requiring the replacement of 212 tiles and the gluing of cracks in approximately 450 others.

JUGENDSTIL AND THE FIRST WORLD WAR: 1895 – 1918

Despite the emergence of new styles and trends in porcelain art at the end of the 19th century, the administration and academic council of the Meissen manufactory remained conservative, adhering to the successful formula of the timeless *old Meissen style.* While art critics faulted Meissen for its failure to lead these artistic developments, the manufactory leadership's stance was commercially sound. This approach maintained a healthy financial position for the manufactory, which enjoyed substantial market demand and was widely regarded as producing some of the highest-quality porcelain paste in Europe. However, Meissen began to lag behind other porcelain producers, such as Royal Copenhagen, Rörstrand, KPM Berlin, and Sèvres, in terms of technological innovation and artistic advancement.[224]

During the Jugendstil or Art Nouveau era, modellers and painters were afforded a degree of creative freedom recalling the 18th century, a period of artistic flourishing at the manufactory. Consequently, despite initial resistance to Art Nouveau ideals, the manufactory administration began exploring new artistic concepts around 1895. Recognizing the need to reassert its artistic position, Meissen could no longer disregard emerging international trends. The preparations for the 1900 Paris exhibition proved to be a turning point. A notable example is Wilhelm

Romanus Georg Andresen, who in 1899, in collaboration with six other modellers, created a series of 12 figurines based on drawings by Maurice Sand (1860).

The innovations of the 1870s and 1880s, which had previously seen limited application, gained prominence during this period. Specifically, coloured glaze, high-temperature underglaze paint, and the pâte-sur-pâte technique became increasingly popular. Further experimentation in the early 20th century aimed to refine these techniques and achieve even greater artistic effects. Within Art Nouveau, technique and artistic expression became more closely integrated, as artists embraced the entire production process as a unified, organic whole. This holistic approach blurred the lines between designing, modelling, painting, and glazing, fostering a new appreciation for materials and a desire to integrate paint and glaze seamlessly with the porcelain paste. Consequently, the decoration (painting and reliefs) was no longer subordinate to the form of the piece, and the conflicts between sculptors and painters, such as those seen between Kändler and Höroldt, were reduced compared to earlier periods.

To stimulate creativity, several strategies were simultaneously employed. The practice of acquiring sculptures from external artists and adapting them for porcelain production, while not new, intensified from 1895 onwards. A notable example and commercial success was the *'Woman with Ball'* (1898), modelled after Walther Schott's (1861-1938) original sculpture. Five years later, his *'Nude Flora'* was also reproduced in porcelain. Otto Pilz (1876-1934) was another significant contributor, creating approximately 30 different models, primarily humorous animal figures. His revised version of the monkey orchestra is particularly notable, featuring nine figurines, each depicting a different monkey species playing an instrument (e.g., a chimpanzee on clarinet, an orangutan on tuba). The polar bear (1903) by Swedish-Austrian sculptor Otto Jarl also gained considerable popularity.

Following the closure of the art/drawing academy in 1893, a revised approach was adopted to cultivate the skills of talented artists. Promising individuals were sent to the Dresden School of Handicrafts or other academies within Germany, with the most exceptional talents given the opportunity to study at academies throughout Europe. The return of these in-house artists injected fresh creativity into the manufactory's traditionally conservative environment. The influence of their studies and work experiences in cities like Paris became increasingly apparent and valued. To further encourage innovation, these artists were granted '*free time*' from their regular duties to develop new works.

In addition, the Meissen manufactory sought to learn directly from its competitors. For instance, Marianne Høst, formerly of the Copenhagen manufactory, worked at Meissen from January 1906 to October 1909. She was among the first women to hold a creative artistic role at Meissen, specializing in underglaze decorations. She primarily produced unique Art Nouveau works, including vases, bowls, and small decorative objects characterised by underglaze painting and naturalistic motifs such as marine life, flowers, and insects. Her contribution lies less in serial production than in the creation of individually designed pieces that reflect the influence of Danish porcelain painting and Jugendstil aesthetics.

Several general trends emerge in porcelain fine arts. While animal art was popular in the 18th century, it was largely forgotten during the Neoclassical and Historicist periods. The Jugendstil movement, however, marked a rebirth. Even in the late 19th century, disputes arose between conservative Historicists and the naturalistic interests of the younger generation. Erich Hösel's (1869-1953) work helped the naturalists prevail, and Paul Walther (1876-1933) became a prominent sculptor.

Beyond animal sculptures, two main figurine types gained popularity during this era. First, there were genre scenes depicting everyday life, such as Konrad Hentschel's child figurines or girls adorned with floral head wreaths. These figurines captured scenes as if drawn directly from everyday life. Second, society fashion figurines were trendy, especially those depicting fashionable women from cities like Berlin or Paris. Karl Theodor Eichler's figurines of actresses, dancers, and other fashionable women exemplify this trend, achieving considerable popularity.[225] For example, in 1911, he created a figurine of Loie (Marie Louise) Fuller, an American dancer renowned for her pioneering work in modern dance and innovative use of light effects. Eichler also produced a notable series of 11 figurines depicting the various professions within the Meissen manufactory.

As the demand for affordable household porcelain grew, the Meissen manufactory aimed to develop modern and inexpensive tableware for the middle class. However, it also continued to produce household porcelain in the traditional Meissen style for wealthier customers. The manufactory engaged several designers to create new sets, but it eventually realized it could not compete with the industrial production of cheap tableware. Its strength lay in manual labour and exclusivity. For instance, the Belgian architect and painter Henry van de Velde created the Whiplash Service in 1903, and Richard Riemerschmid designed the Blue Panicle table set a year later. While original, these services were not commercially successful. The crocus breakfast set (1897) by Konrad Hentschel, the Flügelmuster décor (1901) by his brother Rudolf, the Ahornmuster (1904) by Paul Richter, the Misnia service by Theodor Grust, and the Saxonia Service by Otto Eduard Gottfried Voigt achieved greater success.

Thanks to these artistic and technological developments, Meissen was increasingly perceived as regaining artistic relevance around 1905 and was less frequently criticized for imitating other manufactories. However, this is not to say that Art Nouveau became the sole focus of the Meissen manufactory. Although this *Jugendstil* art may have been of interest to art critics, the wider public and clients were less enthusiastic, and most creations of that time achieved little or no commercial success. Thus, the manufactory sought to balance its heritage with modern art styles. For example, at the Paris Exposition of 1900, approximately 90% of the items on display still conformed to the neoclassical, historicist, and Biedermeier styles. This tension between artistic innovation and commercial conservatism became a defining characteristic of Meissen during this period, shaping both its successes and its limitations.

Many independent artists had limited experience with porcelain, yet they viewed modelling and ornamentation as an integrated process. The resulting works garnered attention at exhibitions and in journals but rarely achieved sustained commercial success, with the exception of some animal sculptures. Thus, the importance of these external artists lies primarily in their influence on in-house artists rather than in their economic impact. From 1906 onward, when the art academy was re-established, the number of outside designers decreased, although some limited collaboration continued for figure and animal sculptures. The Art Nouveau period did not end abruptly, but from 1910 onward, the use of this style and its related techniques gradually but steadily diminished.

The First World War significantly impacted the Meissen manufactory. Approximately one-third of the staff was called into military service, and at one point, the closure of the manufactory was considered. Nevertheless, despite this challenging situation, more than a hundred new models were created, and some 675 older ones were brought back into production.[226] With the abdication of Saxon King Friedrich Augustus III and the transformation of Saxony into a Free State following the end of the First World War, the name of the manufactory changed from Royal Porcelain Manufactory to State Porcelain Manufactory.

THE PFEIFFER ERA: 1919–1934

Appointed Director on 1 November 1918 and General Director in 1926, Max Adolf Pfeiffer (1875-1957) led the Meissen manufactory through a period of significant artistic revival, now commonly referred to as the Pfeiffer Era. This period is widely regarded as one of the most artistically significant periods in the manufactory's history. Some publications narrowly define the Pfeiffer Era as 1924–1934, based on the dot placed between the crossed swords of the trademark during this period, a feature often interpreted—though not universally—as symbolizing a new beginning.

Pfeiffer, a trained mechanical engineer with a strong interest in ceramics and sculpture, had joined the manufactory in 1913 as commercial director. His tenure saw considerable construction and modernization efforts, leading to faster production times. Despite the economic challenges of the era, Pfeiffer contributed to strengthening the manufactory's position among leading European producers.

While the Pfeiffer Era is celebrated for its artistic achievements, it coincided with formidable economic challenges, making Pfeiffer's success all the more remarkable. The hyperinflation following World War I and the global economic crisis after the 1929 crash created an extremely unstable environment for the manufactory. Furthermore, the United States and Japan, formerly major importers of German porcelain, had established their own factories and become global competitors. Many countries also introduced import duties of up to 60%, rendering German porcelain less competitive.

Two centuries after its invention and commercialization by Böttger, the red stoneware had fallen out of favour with customers as white porcelain production increased. Demand dwindled, and the original recipe was no longer fully preserved. However, advancements in chemistry allowed for the analysis of the red stoneware's composition in 1907, sparking interest in William Funk, the manufactory chemist. Funk experimented to recreate a red stoneware similar to Böttger's. In 1919, he achieved a closely comparable result, with feldspar replacing earlier calcium-based components such as alabaster. Martin Mields further refined the paste, and the manufactory named this reinvention *'Böttger stoneware.'* It is sometimes incorrectly referred to as *'Böttger porcelain,'* which specifically refers to the slightly yellowish white porcelain produced before 1721, using alabaster instead of feldspar as a key ingredient.

Pfeiffer envisioned a comprehensive reorganization of the manufactory, encompassing both artistic and structural reforms. He and his colleagues deliberately distanced themselves from Art Nouveau. Consequently, underglaze painting and the pâte-sur-pâte technique declined significantly and were in many cases reduced or discontinued. The elaborate ornamentation of Jugendstil gave way to a more austere and undecorated aesthetic, leading to a resurgence of the sculptural aspect of porcelain art. While the sale of unpainted porcelain had been uncommon throughout most of Meissen's history, it became a significant trend in the 1920s. To prevent the painting of these items outside the manufactory, a special mark was introduced for *'white porcelain.'* Furthermore, numerous new pieces were produced in Böttger stoneware, where —similar to biscuit porcelain—sculptural elements are more prominent due to the absence of glaze.

Pfeiffer aimed to make the manufactory not only economically robust but also artistically exemplary. This dual focus on artistic innovation and economic resilience defined the strategic direction of the manufactory during this period. His strategy involved attracting prominent independent artists to inject fresh creativity into the porcelain art produced within the manufactory. This was particularly important because porcelain art had historically been *'anonymous,'* but collectors were increasingly interested in knowing the artists behind the works. This growing emphasis on artistic authorship also led to the creation of limited-edition *'master pieces,'* produced under the direct supervision of the artist who created the original model.

The new Meissen designs drew inspiration from leading European cultural movements, such as the Deutsche Werkbund in Germany and the Art Deco movement in France. Pfeiffer and many of the artists working for Meissen were members of the Deutsche Werkbund. While the Werkbund's ideas significantly influenced the manufactory, they were not fully implemented. The Werkbund emphasized the form of an object, but Meissen was unwilling to abandon decoration, as its expertise lay in intricate handwork. Consequently, the Pfeiffer era was not defined by a single, unified style. Instead, it showcased a diverse array of individual artistic styles, characterized by variety without extremes. The Pfeiffer era brought about a diversification not only of artistic styles but also of product categories.

Given the economic situation, porcelain remained expensive, which limited the demand for sculptural art. Consequently, the majority of orders at the Meissen manufactory in the 1920s were for tableware. Throughout the 19th century, an increasing number of people had chosen porcelain tableware over wood or metal, a trend that continued into the 1920s. Porcelain offers several advantages: it did not affect the taste of food, retained heat well, was relatively durable and resistant to cutlery damage, and was less porous and more hygienic than many alternative materials. While the household porcelain of the 18th century, particularly Kändler's *'neue Ausschnitt'* design, remained the most commercially successful, three attempts were made to introduce new designs.

The first set was created in 1919 by Adelbert Niemeyer, based on earlier collaborations with the manufactory before the First World War. In line with Werkbund ideals, the tableware's shape and decoration were formal and simple. A second set followed in 1926, designed by Max Esser, who also provided three distinct decoration patterns, one of which was heavily inspired by Art Deco. The final set, created in 1930, is attributed to Paul Börner.

Starting in 1919, a 'Year Plaque' was created in Böttger stoneware and biscuit porcelain. Produced in limited quantities, these plaques were based on the most notable figurine from the preceding year. Although the last Year Plaque dates to 1934, similar jubilee or commemorative plaques have been created since.

The hyperinflation period spurred a novel product line for the Meissen manufactory: *Notgeld*, or emergency money. In 1922-23, the German government struggled to produce sufficient currency, particularly small change. The high rate of inflation meant the metal in coins was often worth more than the coin's nominal value. One solution was to print low-denomination banknotes, but another was to authorize municipalities or companies to issue emergency money in the form of porcelain coins, stamps, coal, wood, and other materials. These could be used as payment locally, but not nationally. The Meissen manufactory was among the entities authorized to produce emergency money, creating coins primarily in Böttger stoneware, and to a lesser extent in white porcelain. The biscuit porcelain coins are slightly smaller than their Böttger stoneware counterparts due to the difference in shrinkage during firing: approximately 16% for biscuit versus around 8–10% for stoneware.[227] These coins, identifiable by the Crossed Swords mark, were produced not only for the city of Meissen, but also for other locations such as Eisenach, Freiberg, Münsterberg, and even Guatemala. Almost all of these coins were designed by in-house artist Emil Paul Börner, who created over a thousand coins, medals, and plaques.[228] Although fragile, these coins became fashionable with collectors, so many were likely never used as currency. Later, medals in Böttger stoneware and porcelain were also produced. However, this did not lead to a new niche market, as Meissen had produced coins in the 18th century, though not for use as currency.

Under Pfeiffer's direction, diversity was prioritized, and more technical products were also explored. In the 1920s, several porcelain stove designs were developed, but their hand-painted decorations made them prohibitively expensive and commercially unviable. Greater success was achieved with technical porcelain, primarily for laboratory use. Porcelain's hardness, fire resistance, and acid resistance are valuable qualities for chemical experiments and industrial applications. While some porcelain producers, such as the Berlin Porcelain Manufactory, derive a significant portion of their revenue from technical porcelain, the production of items such as cupels, crucibles, mortars, pestles, and spot plates remained a marginal activity for Meissen. Due to strong competition, this line of production was discontinued in 1951.

During the Pfeiffer era, the Meissen manufactory commissioned 22 German and Austrian external artists, granting them complete creative freedom. Many of these artists had previously collaborated with Pfeiffer during his tenure as Director in Unterweißbach. Upon his move to Meissen, Pfeiffer leveraged these connections with accomplished independent artists, inviting them to work for Meissen instead. Many of these works achieved significant popularity and remain highly sought after today.

Paul Scheurich (1883-1945) is perhaps the most celebrated of these 22 artists and often regarded as one of the most important porcelain designers after Kändler in the manufactory's history. Over two decades, he created more than a hundred models for Meissen, a remarkable output for an independent artist. His artistic journey was marked by periods of both great creativity and personal hardship. Following a productive early period, he experienced a depression during the First World War. He resumed creating models from 1917 onwards, but the economic crisis of the 1920s further impacted his mental state, which was reflected in his work. Scheurich's early fascination with the world of theatre served as a key source of inspiration for his initial models. For example, in 1913, he created five figurines of dancers from the Russian '*Karnaval*' Ballet, which was touring Europe under the direction of Sergej Djagilev. The collaboration between Scheurich and the Meissen manufactory concluded with Pfeiffer's departure in 1934.

Animal sculptures experienced a resurgence in popularity during the early 20th century. Max Esser emerged as one of the leading external artists creating such figurines for Meissen, employing a level of stylization that was innovative for the manufactory. His animal figures were often left entirely white or only sparsely painted. Esser also created ten animal masks in Böttger stoneware. His '*Otter*', which won a Grand Prix at the 1937 world exhibition in Paris, and '*Seagull on a Wave*' achieved considerable fame. Esser also specialized in chess figurines, a theme Kändler had explored around 1750, but Esser replaced the human figures with animals. One of Esser's masterpieces, and a highlight of the Pfeiffer era, was a table decoration consisting of 75 pieces depicting Goethe's tale of Reynard the Fox, created between 1919 and 1926. This was combined with a table service featuring a Strahlenmuster, which he developed in 1926. In 1929, Esser produced a five-meter tall porcelain cross, constructed in sections, for a newly built church in Berlin. Apart from the gilded nails and the inscription '*INRI*', the cross was left entirely white. Severely damaged during an air raid in the Second World War, it was replaced by a smaller porcelain cross of 67 cm, also by Esser. Other sculptors focusing on animals included August Gaul, known for his monumental style, and Gerhard Marcks, recognized for his high level of stylization.

While less is known about Willi Münch-Khe (1885-1961), his works are artistically remarkable. In 1912-13, before Pfeiffer's arrival at Meissen, Münch-Khe independently developed a series of figurines and Jugendstil decors for wall plates. Recurrent themes included pelicans, peacock feathers, birds, and women dressed in contemporary fashion. A decade later, he received further commissions. From 1925-32, he created animal sculptures and numerous figurines inspired by European literature and fairy tales, executed in both Böttger stoneware and white porcelain, with or without painting. His models of Don Quixote and Sancho Panza, Peter Schlemihl, Till Eulenspiegel, Lamme Goedzak, Simplicius Simplicissimus, and Archivarius Lindhorst have become well-known among collectors.

Ernst Barlach's work represents a complete departure from the Rococo and Jugendstil styles of previous decades. His figurines, characterized by a high level of abstraction, embody a monumental and expressive style.

In addition to collaborations with independent artists, in-house creativity was also stimulated. The most innovative of the Meissen modellers during this period was Emil Paul Börner (1888-1970), previously mentioned for his role in designing coins. He produced a significant number of figurines and vessels, including his simple tableware 'Köln' in 1915, which is one of the earliest modern table services of the manufactory. Börner not only designed the forms but also painted the objects and developed new decors. Perhaps even more important to Meissen's prestige were his contributions to several ambitious projects. From 1920 to 1928, he was in charge of transforming the Saint Nicolas Church in Meissen into a unique memorial site for the First World War, filling it with large statues and wall plates bearing the names of the 1,800 Meissen inhabitants who were casualties of the war. Another achievement by Börner was the creation of what was presented as the first fully functional porcelain carillon. While there are indications that Augustus the Strong ordered a porcelain carillon as early as 1729 and that a table carillon with 48 porcelain bells was created for von Bruhl in 1741, table bells were also produced in the following years.[229] In 1929, to commemorate the millennium anniversary of the city of Meissen, a carillon of 37 white, undecorated bells was installed in the Frauenkirche. Subsequently, more than thirty similar carillons were mounted in German cities, as well as in Poland and Austria.[230]

Most other full-time employees at the manufactory were pre-occupied with other tasks, leaving them little time to create new pieces. Paul Walther had already produced animal figures as early as 1905 in the typical Jugendstil, using underglaze colours as the primary decoration. He remained very active in this field under Pfeiffer's leadership, but the artwork was either left white or painted with overglaze colours. Similarly, Erich Hösel and Erich Oehme found their inspiration in the animal world.

Hösel's importance lies not so much in animal figurines but rather in his attempt to remodel old Meissen figurines according to their originals. As head of the artistic department, he disagreed with Leuteritz' 19th-century approach of adapting the Baroque and Rococo models to contemporary fashion. Even after his retirement in 1929, Hösel continued until 1951 to restore the old forms by referring to the original moulds and Kändler's work reports.

THE CONSEQUENCES OF NATIONAL SOCIALISM AND THE SECOND WORLD WAR: 1934 – 1950

Pfeiffer was placed on leave on 20 May 1933 and ultimately dismissed by the Nazi regime on 31 March 1934. The precise reason for his dismissal remains unclear, but contributing factors may have included poor financial performance, strained relations with Paul Börner, or a perceived failure to adhere to state ideology. Following his dismissal, Pfeiffer relocated to Berlin, where he became associated with the Berlin porcelain manufactory, attracting a number of independent artists to join him. In the subsequent years, the Meissen manufactory was managed by several directors, many of whom had limited artistic training. The exception was Wolfgang Müller von Baczko, a former assistant of Pfeiffer, who was appointed director in November 1936. Von Baczko successfully increased the manufactory's turnover, persuaded some artists who had left with Pfeiffer to return, and secured several international awards. For example, Scheurich's work *'Lady Falling off a Horse'*—along with five other pieces—was sent to the World Exhibition in Paris in 1937, despite being considered morally objectionable by the Nazi regime. The piece received the prestigious Grand Prix, but was not commercialized due to its incompatibility with the political leadership's ideology and standards. Scheurich's reputation was later rehabilitated, and in 1937-38 the manufactory acquired approximately thirty of his new models.[231] Max Esser's famous otter figurine also received a Grand Prix. Von Baczko left in July 1940 under unclear circumstances and was succeeded by Curt Panzer.

Meissen porcelain was popular among the Nazi leadership; Adolf Hitler, for example, is reported to have had a table setting decorated with the red dragon pattern. Foreign Minister von Ribbentrop was also a known porcelain enthusiast and collector. Like most state-controlled industries at the time, the Meissen manufactory was compelled to align with the prevailing ideology, producing Hitler busts, figurines of Hitler Youth and SS troops, as well as coins and plates adorned with swastikas. For instance, Börner created portrait plaques of Hitler and Hindenburg in the early 1930s,[232] and Ernst Seger sculpted a bust of Hitler. However, not all production during this period was overtly ideological; many animal figurines created during these years remain popular and highly regarded. In general, though, overall artistic innovation was constrained, although notable exceptions remained. Artistic freedom was curtailed during the Nazi era, with designs generally subject to approval by the Saxon State Treasury. Therefore, it would be overly simplistic to characterize the manufactory as actively supporting the regime; rather, its production reflects a complex interplay of adaptation, coercion, and institutional survival.

The Second World War profoundly impacted the Meissen manufactory. A portion of its staff was conscripted into the German army, and the gilding process was replaced with yellow paint. Due to material shortages, paints were made with substitutes, resulting in paler, duller colours. Technical porcelain production gained prominence as the manufactory was compelled to produce porcelain spare parts for military equipment. In 1944, a significant portion of the workforce was relocated to manufacture radio and telecommunication devices for the army. Furthermore, a Hungarian fascist armed forces unit was quartered at the manufactory, which reportedly served as a meeting place for security services, Nazi officials, and others.[233]

However, this does not indicate that the Meissen manufactory or its staff embraced a fascist ideology. On the contrary, there are indications that some employees opposed the regime, although open dissent was not possible. Despite the wartime conditions, new works were still created, some of which remain popular today. A prime example is the 'Till Eulenspiegel' figurine, modelled by Alexander Struck in 1941.

As the Eastern Front approached the north of Meissen in late April 1945, and American and British forces launched air raids on the city, the decision was made to move the porcelain collection to the Albrechtsburg's basement for safekeeping. During the war's final days, heavy fighting forced the manufactory to close. This closure prevented human casualties, but heavy artillery caused substantial material damage.

Following the German defeat, local anti-fascist groups assumed control of the city and its assets. After a closure of several weeks, the manufactory resumed operations, albeit on a limited scale. Curt Panzer was dismissed and arrested in mid-May, and reportedly died following mistreatment in custody. An additional 141 staff members suspected of fascist sympathies were also dismissed. The new city administration appointed Herbert Neuhaus as director. Neuhaus was not new to the manufactory, having started as a porcelain painter in 1921 and gradually advancing to a managerial role before being forced to resign in 1933 by the Nazi regime. He promptly contacted the Soviet army and secured protection from First Lieutenant Petrenko amidst the prevailing chaos.[234]

In June 1945, the state of Saxony was placed under the control of the Soviet military administration. Consequently, the Meissen manufactory fell under the purview of Colonel Blochin, who oversaw both the dismantling of equipment used for defence production and the manufactory's reconstruction, a process that took over a year. A key figure in this period was Dr. M. W. Flerow, a ceramist and Soviet major stationed just 15 km from Meissen, who facilitated the acquisition of essential raw materials and coal.[235] Under these challenging circumstances, the manufactory primarily reproduced older models, lacking the resources for new creative endeavours.

As part of war reparations, numerous German factories were dismantled and rebuilt in the Soviet Union. Others, including the Meissen manufactory, were allowed to continue operations but were required to provide their production as restitution. In July 1946, the manufactory was placed under the direct administration of the Soviet company *'Zement.'* While Neuhaus remained in office, he was now subordinate to General-Director N.D. Nikotin, with M. W. Flerow providing support. This restructuring marked a significant increase in activity at the manufactory. Nikotin arranged for the repatriation of Martin Mields, the former technical director, from captivity in Yugoslavia and facilitated the regeneration of equipment. Beyond maximizing war compensations through increased productivity and profit, the Soviet administration sought to establish a new social and economic order in Eastern Germany, rooted in socialist-communist ideology, introducing concepts already prevalent in the Soviet Union. These initiatives included improvements to employee living and working conditions, the establishment of a company kindergarten and sports ground, and the transformation of the manufactory into a cultural hub for Meissen, hosting concerts and exhibitions.[236]

During the manufactory's four years under Soviet control, production primarily focused on tableware, chemical and technical porcelain, with limited output of figurines and other fine art. Notably, there were few new artistic creations during this time.[237] One exception was a large composition titled *'Communist Revolution,'* depicting 23 figures as a tribute to the 1917 October Revolution. This piece was displayed at the Museum of Combat Glory within the Soviet military compound in Dresden but disappeared upon the Soviet Army's withdrawal in 1990.[238] More significant were the works of Alexander Struck, who drew considerable inspiration from animals and fairy tales.

Initially, a large share of production was directed toward Soviet military personnel, but gradually production and exports expanded, with sales primarily managed through the Soviet export society *'Rasno.'*

MEISSEN IN THE GDR: 1950 – 1989

On 7 October 1949, the German Democratic Republic (GDR) was established, and by the spring of 1950, the Meissen porcelain manufactory was transformed into the *'VEB Staatliche Porzellan-Manufaktur Meissen,'* a state-owned enterprise (Volkseigener Betrieb). In 1958, the Soviet Union returned a substantial portion of the porcelain removed from the Albrechtsburg in 1945, along with parts of the Dresden Porcelain Collection, which had suffered a similar fate and is now housed in the Zwinger Palace in Dresden.

Although the company had been restored, it needed to redefine its future direction. With export operations no longer managed through Rasno, Meissen had to reestablish its historical business connections. While challenging initially, these efforts gradually succeeded. The primary export destinations included the Soviet Union and the United States, with Italy, France, Sweden, and Austria also serving as significant markets. Western demand for luxury goods, combined with the GDR's relatively low production costs, supported a period of relative growth. The manufactory's workforce, which had historically ranged between 600 and 900 employees, expanded to more than 1,800.[239] Unlike many enterprises struggling with economic difficulties, the VEB Staatliche Porzellan-Manufaktur Meissen performed comparatively well, generating substantial foreign currency. This development reflects a broader economic paradox of the GDR period: while operating within a socialist system, the manufactory increasingly depended on exports to Western markets, where Meissen porcelain was valued as a luxury product. This dual orientation significantly influenced both production strategies and artistic priorities.

During the 1950s, the manufactory expanded its output to include a range of more affordable and simpler tableware intended for a broader consumer base. Simultaneously, fine arts gradually received renewed attention. In terms of new artistic creations, Meissen primarily focused on producing figurines based on models acquired in the 1930s but never previously rendered in porcelain, as well as newly acquired sculptures, such as the animal figurines of Elfriede Reichel-Drechsler. The manufactory also commercialized new works by Meissen artists, among whom Alexander Struck is particularly notable. He created several figurines inspired by fairy tales and sagas, including Eulenspiegel, Münchhausen on a flying cannonball, Schneider Wibbel, and the Seven Swabians. Stylistically, Meissen production during the GDR period was characterized by a tension between the preservation of historical forms and the introduction of more restrained, modern designs shaped by both contemporary aesthetics and ideological expectations.

The year 1960 marked an important shift for the Meissen manufactory, initiating a revival of artistic creativity alongside substantial changes. In its 250th anniversary year, the manufactory faced new directives from the political leadership, demanding a break from the past to align with prevailing socialist ideologies. The primary objective was to make production more affordable and accessible to the general population. This directive sparked discussions about transitioning from a manufactory to a mechanized factory for mass production. At the same time, traditional artistic motifs associated with feudal and bourgeois culture were to be replaced with designs representative of socialist society. Examples included busts of Lenin and Engels (both 1967, by Peter Strang) and Karl Marx (1953, by Gerhard Bochmann), alongside new figurines depicting workers, pioneer youth, and coins bearing communist and socialist symbols. However, this socialist-themed art did not attract sustained interest from either the general population within the GDR or wealthy international clients.[240]

Another significant event in 1960 was the formation of the *'Collective for Artistic Development'* by designer Ludwig Zepner, sculptor Peter Strang, and painter Heinz Werner. Although initiated a year prior at the request of the trade minister, it was formally established through a charter in June 1966. This infusion of young, in-house talent led to a rapid decline in the practice of commissioning designs from external artists. In 1966, lithographer and flower painter Rudi Stolle joined the Collective to implement Werner's designs, becoming fully integrated in 1970. Volkmar Bretschneider, a painter specializing in flowers and fruit, was the last to join, in 1973.

In 1969, Peter Strang created a parody of Kändler's harlequin series, modelling the five members of the collective dressed as musical clowns. For thirty years, the team enjoyed favourable conditions for fostering their imagination and creativity, designing and modelling new pieces, and exchanging ideas in a dedicated room at Moritzburg Castle (15 km from Meissen). The term *'Collective'* should not be interpreted too literally, as it was more a group of strong individual artists. They created many unique pieces, driven by a growing client demand for artist recognition and exclusivity. The establishment of the Collective thus marked a shift toward institutionalized in-house artistic authorship, replacing the earlier reliance on external designers and reinforcing a more centralized model of creative production.

Still, creativity was somewhat limited, as prior approval was required for any artistic experiment. This approach to artistic development changed after Karl Petermann became the director in 1969. He encouraged the artists to explore porcelain art anew and to produce original pieces. Simultaneously, he supported the manufactory's established traditions. The famous Rococo figurines from the 18th century had been adapted to popular taste in the following century, but Petermann ordered their remodelling to reflect the creators' original intentions. This measure, which encouraged greater artistic experimentation, was welcomed by the Collective. Peter Strang, disliking the seriousness of the socialist sculptures, felt that porcelain was better suited to cheerful and playful themes. Reflecting this, he developed his own style, exemplified by works depicting weddings and clown figures.

In 1973, Ludwig Zepner designed a new service at the request of the GDR government, called the *Large Cutout (Großer Ausschnitt)*, which later became very successful. While not the first table set of the post-war period, none of its predecessors had achieved comparable success. Zepner is often regarded as a key figure in the development of modern Meissen design, and his influence is evident in most vessels created in the second half of the 20th century. He drew inspiration primarily from natural forms, employing flowing contours.[241] While Zepner led in shaping forms, Werner was his counterpart in painting. Stolle and Bretschneider primarily assisted in realizing Werner's designs and projects. Heinz Werner and Rudi Stolle developed the decoration for the *Hunting Service*, which featured hunting scenes rendered in a combination of underglaze and overglaze painting. The artists were allowed to accompany hunters in the forests and fields around Moritzburg Castle, ensuring the accuracy of the hunting scenes.[242] Other decors for the *Large Cutout* are floral compositions and allegorical scenes. During his 36-year career, Werner developed more than 100 different decors, the most famous of which is the *1001 Nights* created in 1967.

Beyond tableware and fine arts for traditional clients, the Meissen manufactory also fulfilled special orders. For example, in 1952, a large porcelain mural was created for the House of Ministries in Berlin. The design of painter Max Lingner was selected and translated into porcelain at Meissen. Fourteen painters, including Heinz Werner and Volkmar Bretschneider, applied the 25-meterwide and 3-meter-tall composition across approximately 1,800 tiles. Similarly, many other murals of smaller sizes were created for schools, government buildings, hotels, and other institutions.

Taken together, these developments illustrate how the Meissen manufactory in the GDR navigated the tensions between tradition, ideology, and international market demands, maintaining its identity while adapting to a fundamentally different political and economic system.

MEISSEN AFTER THE FALL OF THE BERLIN WALL: 1989 – 2008

In early 1989, when Reinhard Fichte, the General Director since 1983, did not return from a trade fair in Frankfurt am Main, Hannes Walter was appointed as his replacement. After German reunification, Fichte returned and unsuccessfully challenged this change in leadership.

A major component of the post-reunification economic reforms was the privatization of state-owned enterprises. The Meissen manufactory was slated to undergo the same process, and the bidding process was already well underway when the Saxon state government intervened. Interested companies included the Japanese conglomerate Mitsubishi and the ceramics company Villeroy & Boch, which had previously exported Meissen products to West Germany. Hannes Walter opposed this privatization and garnered support from Meissen retailers. Kurt Biedenkopf, Saxony's prime minister, recognized the manufactory's cultural significance. Like Augustus the Strong three centuries prior, he understood its impact on Saxony's prestige and reputation. Thus, its status was modernized but it remained under state ownership, with Biedenkopf becoming the chairman of the supervisory board. This period marked a broader transformation in the manufactory's identity, as it repositioned itself within a global luxury market while maintaining its historical legacy.[243] The balance between tradition and innovation became a defining feature of Meissen's post-reunification development.

Despite the significant economic and societal changes following the fall of the Berlin Wall, the manufactory maintained its artistic vision, continuing to reproduce earlier works while also stimulating the creativity of its artists. As a result of economic restructuring and increased competition, layoffs were necessary. Towards the end of the GDR era, the members of the *'Collective for Artistic Development'* were nearing retirement, prompting a generational shift within the manufactory.[244] A new cohort of young artists, including painter Gudrun Gaube, modeller Olaf Fieber, painter Andreas Herten, and modeller Jörg Danielczyk, had been trained by the Collective and ushered in a new wave of creativity. The creation of unique pieces gained further importance during this period, particularly with the proliferation of art galleries in the 1990s.[245]

Aside from tableware and fine art, the Meissen manufactory engaged in a number of technical challenges. It produced clock faces for high-end Glashütte watches, requiring precision work, and cartridge cases for Montblanc fountain pens. Additionally, a new 90-square-meter porcelain mural (one of the largest porcelain murals after the *Fürstenzug*) was created for the Dresden-Neustadt train station. This mural, a masterpiece depicting Saxony's most important castles, necessitated the development of new underglaze paints and a precise cutting technique for the individual plates. Finally, a nearly 300-year-old challenge was overcome with the creation of the first fully functional porcelain organ at Meissen. Johann Joachim Kändler had previously attempted this between 1731 and 1737 in collaboration with the Meissen organ-builder Johann Ernst Hähnel. Their four-meter-tall construction was completed in September 1737, but the sound of the pipes was unclear and inharmonious. This organ, created for the Japanese Palace, is now on display in the Dresden Porcelain Collection. Two pipes created between 1933 and 1945 suggest further attempts to create an organ, possibly by Börner, but these were unsuccessful.[246] Zepner, who grew up in a musical family and played several instruments, strongly believed in the possibilities of porcelain. Inspired by these failed attempts, he decided to create a functional organ with porcelain pipes. Zepner was assisted by the Dresden-based organ producer Jehmlich, which had some prior experience working with porcelain. In 1910, Jehmlich produced an organ with the Teichert porcelain manufactory (located in Meissen), but it served only a decorative purpose, as the pipes, decorated with the blue onion pattern, did not produce sound.[247]

The primary challenge in producing porcelain pipes lies in positioning the sound-producing edge (labium). The volume of the porcelain reduces by approximately 17% during firing. Even when correctly positioned, extensive polishing is required, achievable not through calculations but with the trained ear of an intonator.[248] The organ built in 2000 had 22 porcelain pipes ranging from 48 to 112 cm, as well as 36 wooden and 170 metal pipes. The console was made of pearwood, and the decoration was done by Christoph Ciesielski.

While porcelain may not be immediately associated with modern and experimental art, the Meissen manufactory has also explored this field. A number of younger artists, trained by Meissen's master artisans and influenced by the Collective, began to express their artistic creativity. In doing so, they abandoned strict traditional patterns while retaining their technical skills and commitment to perfection. Most of these modern creations by young artists such as Christoph Ciesielski, Andrea Ehret, Olaf Fieber, and Andreas Herten are unique pieces created without the use of moulds.

The GDR era led to social changes, resulting in increased involvement of women in the creative work of designing new models and patterns. While some progress was visible in the 1980s, it was only after the fall of the Berlin Wall that women assumed leading roles. Three women, in particular, stand out: Silvia Klöde, Sabine Wachs, and Gudrun Gaube.

Silvia Klöde initially focused on creating new medals but gradually transitioned to designing figurines. Women frequently occupy a central position in her works, consistently depicted as independent, wilful, and self-conscious personalities who radiate friendliness, cheerfulness, humanity, and optimism.[249] She developed a distinctive approach to the portrait bust, exemplified by 'Bal parè' (1990-91) and 'Dame mit Hut' (1991). In subsequent years, she also created a wide range of decorated mirrors, vases, boxes, terrines, and other items.[250]

Sabine Wachs joined the Meissen porcelain manufactory in 1985 and has since designed a significant number of unique porcelain art objects. After creating a coffee service with a modern décor in the early 1990s, Wachs was commissioned in 1993 to create a large coffee, tea, and dinner service, but within the constraints of the conservative Meissen style.[251] This 'Waves' Service, available in both 'pure' and 'with relief' versions, was finalized with the assistance of Joerg Danielczyk and other colleagues. While also available in white, the decors used to decorate the 'Waves' service make it particularly appealing to the contemporary market. Wachs also created the 'Forest flora with insects' decor herself. Visitors to the Meissen manufactory will notice the 36 by 12-meter façade at the entrance of the visitor's centre. Created by Wachs in collaboration with the painter Annett Waldeck, it combines porcelain and photo concrete.[252] This project led to a new application of porcelain in interior design and architecture.

Gudrun Gaube joined the manufactory in 1990 to design new decors and contribute to unique pieces. Her deep study of nature is evident in her paintings of flora and fauna, and she even developed a new style of flower painting.[253] Rather than presenting idealized images, she depicted the natural cycle of flowers, from seedling to plant, bud to blossom, and eventual fading and withering.[254] She created several decors for tableware designed by Wachs, including 'Floral Tendril,' 'Scattered Flowers,' 'Blue Hydrangea,' 'Venetian Journey,' and the Christmas-inspired 'Holly' for the Waves Service.

Another key figure is Jörg Danielczyk, who began his training as a bosserer at the manufactory in 1969 and became a modeller in 1973. From 1978, he was part of Peter Strang's Collective. Danielczyk later earned degrees in sculpture in Dresden and vessel design in Halle.

MEISSEN IN THE 21ST CENTURY: FROM PORCELAIN TO LIFESTYLE LUXURY BRAND

Over the past three centuries, the porcelain market has experienced numerous fluctuations, with many manufactories failing to weather these challenges. Towards the 21st century, global demand for traditional luxury tableware and porcelain figurines showed signs of decline, significantly impacting the turnover and profitability of manufactories, including Meissen. Despite the survival of only a few manufactories compared to the numerous industrial factories, Meissen has focused on securing its long-term future. The appointment of Christian Kurtzke as CEO signalled a new era. Kurtzke's strategy for Meissen's future development centred on innovation while honouring tradition. This involved adopting a fresh approach to artistic creativity and diversifying the product range. Consequently, Kurtzke aimed to transform Meissen from a porcelain manufactory into a high-end lifestyle brand. Under the motto "Pioneers move on, settlers build further," he departed seven years later. This transformation reflects a broader structural shift in the luxury goods sector in the early 21st century, in which heritage manufacturers increasingly redefined themselves as brands rather than solely as producers. In this context, Meissen sought to reposition itself within the global luxury market, operating at the intersection of craftsmanship, design, and brand identity. This transition introduced a fundamental tension between preserving artisanal authenticity and adapting to the demands of contemporary luxury consumption.

Instead of relying solely on in-house modellers to inject new creative energy into porcelain art, Kurtzke revitalized the system of engaging external artists for shorter residencies or specific assignments, echoing Pfeiffer's approach a century prior. Kurtzke aimed to reinvigorate artistic development in porcelain art and reinforce Meissen's position as a leading manufacturer. To this end, he established an Art Campus in 2009, offering promising artists —many of whom lacked extensive experience with the nuances of porcelain—the opportunity to stimulate their imaginations and cultivate new skills, ultimately leading to innovative creations. Over thirty artists from Europe, the US, the Middle East, and Asia have participated in this initiative. However, in contrast to Pfeiffer, Kurtzke placed less emphasis on in-house artistic production, and the contracts of Klöde, Wachs, and Gaube were terminated in August 2010, leaving Danielczyk as the sole remaining modeller. This restructuring marked a decisive break with the institutional model that had defined Meissen throughout the 20th century. Whereas earlier periods relied on stable in-house artistic communities, Kurtzke's approach prioritized flexibility, international collaboration, and project-based creativity. While this strategy aligned with contemporary practices in the global art and design world, it also raised concerns about the erosion of continuity in traditional craftsmanship and institutional knowledge.

One of the most renowned and successful of these external artists is the young American ceramist Chris Antemann, whose work has been exhibited extensively throughout Europe and the US and is featured in numerous museums. Heavily inspired by 18th-century porcelain art, particularly the interplay between male and female roles, Antemann's creations at the Meissen Art Campus often narrate stories, frequently in the form of parody, addressing specific social issues without shying away from taboos. The fusion of 18th-century Baroque and Rococo styles with modern stylistic elements renders her work highly distinctive. While she adorns the dresses of her figurines with the same flowers as her predecessors did nearly three centuries earlier, her figures are more scantily clad. Her "Forbidden Fruit" collection, inspired by Kändler's works, comprises numerous sculptures depicting Antemann's interpretation of the Garden of Eden. For example, her "Love Temple" is based on a creation by Kändler from around 1750 and even bears the same name, featuring a dinner party scene inside with lightly dressed ladies seated not only around but also atop the table.[255] Her work illustrates how Meissen's historical visual language could be reinterpreted for a contemporary audience, transforming Rococo aesthetics into a medium for modern narrative and social commentary.

Ukraine-born architect Vladimir Kanevsky began working with ceramics in his twenties. After emigrating to the US in 1989, he established his own porcelain workshop. Initially creating naturalistic tableware, he gradually focused on crafting flowers from his preferred material. Given porcelain's fragility, Kanevsky adopted an architectural approach, combining it with metal for stems and copper for leaves. Each flower is unique, as Kanevsky makes them all by hand. His work gained international recognition, including interest from luxury houses such as Dior. In 2012, as part of Meissen's Art Campus project, he created a collection of 11 pieces, making the flowers appear remarkably realistic and detailed, complete with insect bites, broken stems, and discoloured patches on the leaves.

This renewed interest in porcelain flowers has deep historical roots within the Meissen tradition. Kanevsky was not the first to create porcelain flowers. While Kändler produced porcelain flowers as early as 1746, even recruiting Johann Georg Janicke the following year to focus solely on this,[256] the Vincennes manufactory in France excelled in this art form during the 1740s. Two years after receiving a Meissen wedding gift from her father, Augustus III, Maria Josepha, who had married the French crown prince, sent a stunning bouquet of 460 Vincennes (soft-paste) porcelain flowers to her father.[257] This inspired the Meissen manufactory to enhance its own creations in this area, establishing a leading position in the 1750s.[258] Kanevsky's work demonstrates how traditional technical expertise can be reframed within a contemporary design context, appealing to collectors beyond the conventional porcelain market.

However, this did not diminish the importance of Meissen's own artists. In 2014, Jörg Danielczyk celebrated the upcoming 25th anniversary of German reunification by creating a life-size figurine called *'Saxonia,'* demonstrating Meissen's continued leadership in porcelain art. In creating this largest freestanding porcelain statue in the world (180 cm tall and 800 kg), Danielczyk pushed the technical limits of porcelain. The figure is adorned with Meissen jewellery and a dress covered in 8,000 snowball blossoms, a clear reference to Kändler's legacy. The firing process took three weeks, and the statue consists of two pieces stacked on top of each other. This work is notable not only for its impressive dimensions but also for its artistic qualities. The sculptor depicted Kurtzke's vision of *'innovating while respecting traditions.'* This *'Saxon Statue of Liberty,'* as Kurtzke described it, features a Chanel model, alluding to Meissen's initial foray into the world of couture, as well as Danielczyk's newfound passion for the catwalk and his collaboration with Karl Lagerfeld. Danielczyk had already created porcelain items incorporated into the Chanel collection in 1998. The figure can be interpreted as a symbolic statement of Meissen's identity in the early 21st century—combining historical references, technical ambition, and engagement with contemporary fashion and luxury culture.

In 2009, Meissen expanded its activities into architectural ceramics, focusing on the production of durable, high-quality porcelain tiles for interior and exterior applications. These materials were used in luxury hospitality environments, including projects associated with hotel groups such as Kempinski and Ritz-Carlton, as well as in private residences and commercial interiors. This development reflects a broader trend in the luxury sector, where heritage brands extend their expertise into architectural and spatial design, thereby integrating craftsmanship into everyday environments beyond traditional decorative objects.

As part of its ambition to evolve into a lifestyle brand, Meissen expanded beyond porcelain production to encompass other segments of the luxury industry, aiming to broaden its clientele. This was not entirely new. During the era of Augustus the Strong, when gold and porcelain were similarly priced, Meissen produced jewellery with porcelain inlays. In 2010, Meissen revived this tradition, introducing several jewellery collections under the "Meissen Joaillerie" label. These collections draw heavily on traditional Meissen motifs. For instance, the "1739 Royal Blossom Collection" incorporates Kändler's snowball blossom motif, the "1722 Swords" collection is based on the Crossed Swords trademark symbol, and the "Royal Mystery" collection features painted porcelain inlays. This expansion into jewellery illustrates how Meissen translated its historical visual language into wearable objects, thereby extending its brand identity into new domains while maintaining continuity with its decorative heritage.

Moving further afield, Meissen also developed couture and furniture collections. Since 2012, scarves, ties, handbags, and silk dresses were produced through Meissen Italia, a subsidiary based in Milan. This line also included home décor items such as carpets, tables, chairs, armchairs, and cushions. Despite the distance from pure porcelain production, these new objects maintained a connection to Meissen's 300-year heritage. They were often inspired by patterns and decors used in porcelain decoration or by the history of the Albrechtsburg. For example, cushions were adorned with flowers commonly used for tableware decoration or drawings by Adam von Löwenfinck, scarves were decorated with Ming Dragons, and carpets feature designs mirroring the original floors of the Albrechtsburg. Through these initiatives, Meissen increasingly positioned itself not merely as a manufacturer of objects, but as a comprehensive luxury brand. This shift aligned it with other heritage houses in Europe that have expanded into lifestyle sectors, where brand identity and narrative play a central role in value creation.

Since the departure of Christian Kurtzke in 2013, the Meissen Manufactory has entered a more cautious and, in many respects, consolidative phase. Kurtzke's tenure had been defined by an ambitious attempt to reposition Meissen as a broader luxury lifestyle brand, expanding beyond porcelain into areas such as fashion, interior design, and accessories. While this strategy generated visibility and briefly aligned Meissen with contemporary luxury branding trends, it also exposed the manufactory to financial strain and criticism for diluting its core identity.

In the period following his departure, Meissen appears to have refocused on its historical strengths—namely, high-quality porcelain production rooted in craftsmanship, technical mastery, and artistic continuity. The emphasis has shifted back toward limited-edition objects, collector-oriented figurines, and refined tableware, often drawing on the manufactory's extensive archive of 18th-century models. This return to tradition is not purely conservative; rather, it reflects a strategic recalibration in response to a global market that increasingly values authenticity, provenance, and artisanal excellence over brand diversification.

At the same time, the manufactory continues to navigate structural challenges common to heritage luxury producers. Demand for traditional porcelain remains uneven, particularly among younger consumers, and competition from both high-end design brands and mass-market producers persists. In this context, Meissen has pursued a more measured form of innovation—collaborations with contemporary artists, selective reinterpretations of historic forms, and a careful integration of modern aesthetics into its product lines—without fully abandoning its identity as Europe's oldest porcelain manufactory.

Overall, the post-Kurtzke era can be understood as a period of strategic retrenchment and identity clarification. Rather than pursuing rapid expansion, Meissen has sought to stabilize its position by reaffirming the values that historically defined its prestige: continuity of production, artistic excellence, and the enduring symbolic capital of the crossed swords mark.

Taken together, these developments illustrate a profound transformation in Meissen's identity in the early 21st century. While rooted in a tradition of technical mastery and artistic excellence, the manufactory increasingly adapted to the dynamics of a global luxury market, where brand, narrative, and cross-disciplinary design play a decisive role. This evolution brought new opportunities for innovation and visibility, but also introduced tensions between heritage and commercialization that continue to shape Meissen's trajectory.

USED LITERATURE

Adams, Yvonne. *Meissen Figures 1730-1775: The Kaendler Years*. Atlgen, PA: Schiffer Publishing, 2007.

Berling, Karl. *Königlich Sächsische Porzellanmanufactur Meissen: 1710 – 1910*. Leipzig: F A Brockhaus, 1911.

Beyer, Uwe. Meissener *Wandbilder 1976 bis 1992: Heinz Werner, Rudi Stolle, Volkmar Bretschneider, Jörg Danielczyk, Horst Bretschneider*. Meissen: Staatliche Porzellan-Manufaktur Meissen, 1992.

Beyer, Uwe. *Peter Strang: Porzellanplastiker aus Leidenschaft, Meissener Manuskripte*. Meissen: Staatliche Porzellan-Manufaktur Meissen, 2001.

Beyer, Uwe. *Einen Pfau in Lebens Groesse Modelliret...: Meissener Manuskripte XIX*. Meissen: Staatliche Porzellan-Manufaktur Meissen, 2006.

Borrmann, Antje, Finger, Birgit, and Schellenberger (eds.) Simona. *Kunst oder Kommerz?: Meissener Porzellan im 19. Jahrhundert*. Dresden: Staatliche Schlösse, Burgen und Gärten Sachsen: Sandstein, 2010.

Brattig, Patricia (ed.). *Meissen: Barockes Porzellan*. Stuttgart: Arnoldsche Verlagsanstalt, 2010.

Braun, Peter. *Form vollendet: Meissener Manuskripte XVIII*. Meissen: Staatliche Porzellan-Manufaktur Meissen, 2006.

Britzke, Brigitte. *Friedrich der Große und seine Porzellanbestellungen in Meißen während des Siebenjährigen Krieges*. Bad Pyrmont: Museumsverein im Schloss Pyrmont e.V., 2012.

Cassidy-Geiger, Maureen. "Meissen et la France avant et après la Guerre de Sept ans: Artistes, Espionnage et Commerce." In XXes Rencontres de l'Ecole du Louvre: Art français et art allemand au XVIIIe siècle – regards croisés (Paris, 2008): 61-99.

Chilton, Meredith. *Fired by Passion*. Stuttgart: Arnoldsche Verlagsanstalt, 2009.

Creighton, Charles. *The fabulous Meissen apostles*. Place of publication and publisher not identified, 1978.

Dämmig, Helmut. *Meißner Porzellanglockenspiele*. Meissen: Thieme, 1987.

Davies, Hugh Marlais and Sonntag, Hans. *Meissen Porcelain Dogs: Meissener Porzellanhunde 1875-1925*. London: Hugh Davies Publishing, 1997.

Eberle, Martin. Cris de Paris. Meissener Porzellanfiguren des 18. Jahrhunderts / Meissen Porcelain Figurines of the 18th Century. Leipzig: Gohliser Schlösschen, 2001.

Eikelmann, Renate (ed.). *Meißener Porzellan des 18. Jahrhunderts: Die Stiftung Ernst Schneider in Schloß Lustheim*. München: Hirmer, 2013.

Finlay, Robert. *The Pilgrim Art: Cultures of Porcelain in World History*. Berkeley: University of California Press, 2010.

Geiger, Maureen C. *Fragile Diplomacy: Meissen Porcelain for European Courts: Meissen Porcelain for European Courts, 1710-1763*. New York: Yale University Press, 2008.

Gleeson, Janet. *The Arcanum: Extraordinary True Story of the Invention of European Porcelain*. London: Bantam, 1997.

Harris Cohen, David and Hess, Catherine. *Looking at European Ceramics: A Guide to Technical Terms*. Malibu, CA: J. Paul Getty Museum, 1993.

Jedding, Hermann. *Meißener Porzellan des 19. und 20. Jahrhunderts 1800 - 1933. Bestimmen, bewerten, erhalten*. München: Keysersche Verlagsbuchhandlung, 1993.

Just, Johannes. *Meissen porcelain and the art nouveau period*. Cincinnati: Seven Hills Books, 1985.

Keisch, Christiane. *Meissen heute ,Arbeiten des Künstlerkollektivs Ludwig Zepner, Peter Strang, Heinz Werner, Rudi Stolle, Volkmar Bretschneider*. Berlin: Staatliche Museen zu Berlin, 1976.

Keramos: Zeitschrift der Gesellschaft der Keramikfreunde. Düsseldorf: Gesellschaft der Keramikfreunde, 1958–2022.

Kisluk-Grosheide, Daniëlle O. "The reign of magots and pagods." *Metropolitan Museum Journal* 37 (2002): 177-198.

Lübke, Diethard. *Das Grabowski-Service*. Bramsche: Rasch, 2011.

Lübke, Diethard. *Chinesische Nachahmungen von Meißner Porzellan*. Bramsche: Rasch, 2012.

Lübke, Diethard. *Meißner Watteau-Malerei aus dem 18. Jahrhundert*. Bramsche: Rasch, 2013.

Lübke, Diethard. *Das Meißner Tee-, Kaffee- und Schokoladenservice des Kölner Kurfürsten Clemens August*. Bramsche: Rasch, 2013.

Lübke, Diethard. *Meissner Porzellan mit ostasiatischen Dekoren: Beiträge zur Deutung von 35 ostasiatischen Porzellandekoren aus dem 18. Jahrhundert*. Bramsche: Rasch, 2014.

Lübke, Diethard. *Keramische Fachbegriffe für die Analyse von frühem Meißner Porzellan*. Bramsche: Rasch, 2014.

Lübke, Diethard. *Johann Gottlieb Mehlhorn*. Bramsche: Rasch, 2015.

Lübke, Diethard. *George Funcke*. Bramsche: Rasch, 2015.

Marryat, Joseph. *A History of Pottery and Porcelain, Mediæval and Modern*. London: J. Murray, 1857.

Marush-Krohn, Caren. *Meissener Porzellan 1918–1933: Die Pfeifferzeit*. Leipzig: Edition Leipzig, 1993.

Menzhausen, Ingelore. *Early Meissen Porcelain in Dresden*. New York: Thames & Hudson Ltd, 1990.

Menzhausen, Ingelore. Alt - Meißner Porzellan in Dresden. Augsburg: Weltbild, 1994.

Menzhausen, Ingelore and Karpinski, Jürgen. *In Porzellan verzaubert: die Figuren Johann Joachim Kändlers in Meissen aus der Sammlung Pauls-Eisenbeiss Basel*. Basel: Wiese, 1993.

Miedtank, Lutz. *Zwiebelmuster*. Leipzig: Edition Leipzig, 1991.

Morley-Fletcher, Hugo. *Meissen Porcelain in Colour*. Exeter: Exeter Books, 1979.

Pietsch, Ulrich. *Schwanenservice: Meissener Porzellan für Heinrich Graf von Brühl*. Berlin: Edition Leipzig, 2000.

Pietsch, Ulrich (ed.) *Meissen for the czars: porcelain as a means of Saxon-Russian politics in the eighteenth century*. München: Hirmer, 2004.

Pietsch, Ulrich. *Die figürliche Meissner Porzellanplastik von Gottlieb Kirchner und Johann Joachim Kaendler: Bestandskatalog der*

Porzellansammlung Staatliche Kunstsammlungen Dresden. München: Hirmer, 2006.

Pietsch, Ulrich and Ufer, Peter. *Mythos Meissen: das erste Porzellan Europas*. Dresden: Ed. Sächs. Zeitung, 2008.

Pietsch, Ulrich. *Zauber der Zerbrechlichkeit: Meisterwerke europäischer Porzellankunst*. Leipzig: Seemann, 2010.

Pietsch, Ulrich. *Passion for Meissen: Marouf Collection*. Stuttgart: Arnoldsche Verlagsanstalt, 2010.

Pietsch, Ulrich and Banz, Claudia (eds.) *Triumph of the Blue Swords: Meissen Porcelain for Aristocracy and Bourgeoisie, 1710–1815*. Leipzig: Seemann E.a., 2010.

Pietsch, Ulrich. *Phantastische Welten: Malerei auf Meissener Porzellan und deutschen Fayencen von Adam Friedrich von Löwenfinck (1714-1754)*. Stuttgart: Arnoldsche Verlagsanstalt, 2014.

Röbbig, Gerhard. *Cabinet Pieces: The Meissen Porcelain Birds of Johann Joachim Kändler*. Munich: Hirmer Verlag Gmbh, 2008.

Röntgen, Robert E. *The Book of Meissen*. Exton, PA: Schiffer Pub Ltd, 1996.

Rückert, Rainer. *Biographische Daten der Meißener Manufakturisten des 18. Jahrhunderts. Katalog der Meißener Porzellan-Sammlung Stiftung Ernst Schneider Schloß Lustheim, Oberschleißheim bei München*. München: Bayerisches Nationalmuseum, 1990.

Schärer, Jürgen. *Von Wegen: Meissener Manuskripte Sonderheft II*. Meissen: Staatliche Porzellanmanufaktur, 1992.

Scheuch, Karl. *Münzen aus Porzellan und Ton der Staatlichen Porzellanmanufaktur Meissen und anderer Keramischen Fabriken des In- und Auslandes*. Gütersloh: Strothotte Verlag, 2012.

Schnorr von Carolsfeld, Ludwig. *Porzellan der europäischen Fabriken des 18. Jahrhunderts*. Berlin: Richard Carl Schmidt & Co, 1912.

Schuster, Bettina. *Meissen. Geschichten zur Geschichte und Gegenwart der ältesten Porzellanmanufaktur Europas*. Wien: P. Neff Verlag, 1993.

Schuster, Bettina. *Volkmar Bretschneider; Dekorationen auf Meissener Porzellan*. Meissen: Staatliche Porzellan-Manufaktur Meissen, 1995.

Sonntag, Hans. *Museum. Schauhalle Staatliche Porzellan-Manufaktur Meissen*. Braunschweig: Westermann, 1991.

Sonntag, Hans (ed.). *Die Affenkapelle aus Meissener Porzellan.* Frankfurt am Main: Insel, 1993.

Sonntag, Hans and Karpinski, Jürgen. *Die Sprache der Blumen. Meissener Porzellan.* Leipzig: Seemann, 1995.

Sonntag, Hans and Karpinski, Jürgen. *Erlebte Kunst: Meissener Figurenporzellan aus drei Jahrhunderten.* Leipzig: Edition Leipzig, 1997.

Sonntag, Hans and Karpinski, Jürgen. *Meissener Porzellan.* Leipzig: Edition Leipzig, 1998.

Sonntag, Hans. *Die Botschaft des Drachen: Ostasiatische Glückssymbole auf Meissener Porzellan.* Leipzig: Edition Leipzig, 1999.

Sonntag, Hans and Karpinski, Jürgen. *Verwandlungen, Literarische Figuren in Meissener Porzellan.* Leipzig: Edition Leipzig, 1999.

Staatliche Kunstsammlungen Dresden. *Liebe, Moral und Sentiment: Das Meissner Porzellan mit dem Stern.* Cottbus: Regia Verlag, 2005.

Staatliche Porzellan-Manufaktur Meissen. *250 Jahre Staatliche Porzellan-Manufaktur Meissen.* Meissen: VEB Staatliche Porzellanmanufaktur Meissen, 1960.

Staatliche Porzellan-Manufaktur Meissen. *Meissener Konturen 1960-1990. Porzellane von Ludwig Zepner, Heinz Werner, Peter Strang, Rudi Stolle, Volkmar Bretschneider.* Leipzig: Edition Leipzig, 1991.

Staatliche Porzellan-Manufaktur Meissen. *Forbidden Fruit.* Hamburg: United Verlag und Agentur, 2013.

Stahlbusch, Till Alexander. *Weißes Gold aus Meißen. Service und Geschirre: Service und Geschirre.* Regenstauf: Battenberg Verlag Label der H.Gietl Verlag & Publikationsservice, 2009.

Sterba, Günther. *Gebrauchsporzellan aus Meissen.* Leipzig: Edition Leipzig, 1988.

Sterba, Günther. *Meissener Tafelgeschirr.* Stuttgart: Deutsche Verlags-Anstalt, 1989.

VEB Staatliche Porzellan-Manufaktur Meißen. *Aus ihrer Geschichte und ihrem Schaffen.* Meissen: VEB Staatliche Porzellan-Manufaktur Meißen, 1973.

Von Spee, Pauline Gräfin. *Die klassizistische Porzellanplastik der Meissener Manufaktur von 1764 bis 1814.* Unpublished doctoral dissertation, Rheinische Friedrich-Wilhelms-Universität Bonn, 2004.

Walcha, Otto. *Meissner Porzellan – Von den Anfängen bis zur Gegenwart.* Dresden: Verlag der Kunst, 1973.

Wills, John. E. Jr. *China and Maritime Europe, 1500-1800: Trade, Settlement, Diplomacy, and Missions.* Cambridge: Cambridge University Press, 2011.

Willsberger, Johan and Rückert, Rainer. *Meissen. Porzellan des 18. Jahrhunderts.* Regensburg: Walhalla und Praetoria, 2002.

Wittwer, Samuel. *A Royal Menagerie: Meissen Porcelain Animals.* Los Angeles, CA: Getty Trust Publications, 2001.

Wittwer, Samuel. *The Gallery of Meissen Animals: Augustus the Strong's Menagerie for the Japanese Palace in Dresden.* Munich: Hirmer, 2006.

Zimmerman, Ernst. *Die Erfindung und Frühzeit des Meissner Porzellans: ein Beitrag zur Geschichte der Deutschen Keramik.* Berlin: Georg Reimer, 1908.

---

[1] Ulrich Pietsch and Peter Ufer, *Mythos Meissen: das erste Porzellan Europas* (Dresden: Ed. Sächs. Zeitung, 2008), 39.

[2] Otto Walcha, *Meissner Porzellan – Von den Anfängen bis zur Gegenwart* (Dresden: Verlag der Kunst, 1973), 19.

[3] Ludwig Schnorr von Carolsfeld, *Porzellan der europäischen Fabriken des 18. Jahrhunderts* (Berlin: Richard Carl Schmidt & Co, 1912), 26.

[4] Siegfried Asche, "Die Dresdner Bildhauer des frühen achtzehnten Jahrhunderts als Meister des Böttgersteinzeugs und des Böttgerporzellans," *Keramos* 49 (1970): 67.

[5] Günter Reinheckel, "Plastische Dekorationsformen im Meisner Porzellan des 18. Jahrhunderts," *Keramos* 41-42 (1968): 10.

[6] Otto Walcha, 22.

[7] Günter Reinheckel, "Johann Jakob Irminger," *Keramos* 21 (1963): 14.

[8] Ibid, 16.

[9] Ludwig Schnorr von Carolsfeld, 13-14.

[10] Günter Reinheckel, "Johann Jakob Irminger," *Keramos* 21 (1963): 18-20.

[11] Otto Walcha, 35.

[12] Günter Reinheckel, "Plastische Dekorationsformen im Meisner Porzellan des 18. Jahrhunderts," *Keramos* 41-42 (1968): 19.

[13] Ibid, 28.

[14] Robert E. Röntgen, *The Book of Meissen* (Exton, PA: Schiffer Pub Ltd, 1996), 143.

[15] Daniëlle O. Kisluk-Grosheide, "The reign of magots and pagods," *Metropolitan Museum Journal* 37 (2002): 177.

[16] Ibid., 184.

[17] Siegfried Asche, "Die Dresdner Bildhauer des frühen achtzehnten Jahrhunderts als Meister des Böttgersteinzeugs und des Böttgerporzellans," *Keramos* 49 (1970): 67.

[18] Ursel Berger and Volker Krahn, "Ein Modell von Balthasar Permoser für eine Figur in Böttgersteinzeug," *Keramos* 101 (1983): 6-7.

[19] Siegfried Asche, *Balthasar Permoser* (Berlin, 1978), 124.

[20] See, for example, Siegfried Asche, "Die Dresdner Bildhauer des frühen achtzehnten Jahrhunderts als Meister des Böttgersteinzeugs und des Böttgerporzellans," *Keramos* 49 (1970): 69.

[21] Ibid., 69-70.

[22] Ibid., 70.

[23] Ibid., 83-84.

[24] Ibid., 74.

[25] Ibid., 79.

[26] Ibid., 81-82.

[27] See Ingelore Menzhausen, *Early Meissen Porcelain in Dresden* (New York: Thames & Hudson Ltd, 1990), 226, and Ursel Berger and Volker Krahn, "Ein Modell von Balthasar Permoser für eine Figur in Böttgersteinzeug," *Keramos* 101 (1983): 12. Contrary to Menzhausen, Gertrud Rudloff-Hille and Hilde Rakebrand argue that all six figures should be ascribed to Paul Heerman (Gertrud Rudloff-Hille and Hilde Rakebrand, "Die Gothaer Komödienfiguren," *Keramos* 36 (1967): 3-17). Asche attributed them to Johann Joachim Kretzschmar (Siegfried Asche, "Die Dresdner Bildhauer des frühen achtzehnten Jahrhunderts als Meister des Böttgersteinzeugs und des Böttgerporzellans," *Keramos* 49 (1970): 85).

[28] Ursel Berger and Volker Krahn, 12-13.

[29] See, for example, Ingrid Wildtraut und Helmut Buchen, "Das Commedia dell'Arte-Service. Eine Einführung in eine Gruppe früherer Höroldt-Dekore," *Keramos* 156 (1997): 3-28.

[30] Horst Mauter, "Zur Geschichte der 'Porzellanmanufaktur' in Plaue an

der Havel 1713-1730," *Keramos* 182 (2003): 55.

[31] Ibid, 56.

[32] Ibid, 60.

[33] Günter Reinheckel, "Johann Jakob Irminger," *Keramos* 21 (1963): 21.

[34] Richard Seyffarth, "Johann Gregorius Höroldt Fecit?," *Keramos* 3 (1959): 24-25.

[35] Gerhard Röbbig, *Cabinet Pieces: The Meissen Porcelain Birds of Johann Joachim Kändler* (Munich: Hirmer Verlag GmbH, 2008), 26.

[36] Richard Seyffarth, "Die Porzellanmalerei in der Höroldtzeit," *Keramos* 50 (1970): 133.

[37] Otto Seitler, "Email- und Porzellanmalereien des Christian Friedrich Herold," *Keramos* 6 (1959): 20-26.

[38] See, for example, T.H. Clarke, "Eine Meisen-Entdeckung - Sabina Auffenwerth in Augsburg," *Keramos* 60 (1973): 17-40.

[39] Rainer Rückert, "Zur Staffierung der Gesichter von Meißener Porzellanfiguren - Teil I," *Keramos* 149 (1995): 32.

[40] This codex is kept in the Grassi Museum in Leipzig and was published in 2010 by Hirmer Verlag (Munich) under the title *Exotische Welten: Der Schulz-Codex und das frühe Meissener Porzellan.*

[41] Richard Seyffarth, "Die Porzellanmalerei in der Höroldtzeit," *Keramos* 50 (1970): 132.

[42] Ibid., 132.

[43] Diethard Lübke's *Meißner Porzellan mit ostasiatischen Dekoren* provides an overview of 35 East Asian decors and explains the symbolism of each.

[44] Diethard Lübke, *Meissner Porzellan mit ostasiatischen Dekoren* (Bramsche: Rasch, 2014), 32.

[45] Diethard Lübke describes the Meissen peculiarities of these Chinese imitations in *Chinesische Nachahmungen von Meißner Porzellan* (Bramsche: Rasch, 2012).

[46] Ulrich Pietsch and Claudia Banz (eds.) *Triumph of the Blue Swords: Meissen Porcelain for Aristocracy and Bourgeoisie, 1710–1815* (Leipzig: Seemann E.a., 2010), 53.

[47] Rainer Rückert, "Zur Staffierung der Gesichter von Meißener Porzellanfiguren - Teil I," *Keramos* 149 (1995): 30.

[48] Günter Reinheckel, "Die erste Folge der Pariser Ausrufer in Meißner

Porzellan," *Keramos* 50 (1970): 116.

[49] See for example T. H. Clarke, "Equestrian and other dwarfs on early Meissen porcelain / Reitende und andere Zwerge auf frühem Meißen-Porzellan," *Keramos* 119 (1988): 6-57.

[50] Ludwig Schnorr von Carolsfeld, *Porzellan der europäischen Fabriken des 18. Jahrhunderts* (Berlin: Richard Carl Schmidt & Co, 1912), 37.

[51] Victor Böhmert cited in Günter Reinheckel, "Plastische Dekorationsformen im Meisner Porzellan des 18. Jahrhunderts," *Keramos* 41-42 (1968): 10.

[52] Samuel Wittwer, *A Royal Menagerie: Meissen Porcelain Animals* (Los Angeles, CA: Getty Trust Publications, 2001), 3.

[53] Ibid, 9.

[54] Ibid, 13.

[55] Ingelore Menzhausen and Jürgen Karpinski, *In Porzellan verzaubert* (Basel: Wiese, 1993), 14-15.

[56] Günher Reinheckel, "Ein Uhrgehäuse aus Meißner Porzellan von Johann Gottlieb Kirchner," *Keramos* 26 (1964): 6-10.

[57] Ingelore Menzhausen and Jürgen Karpinski, *In Porzellan verzaubert* (Basel: Wiese, 1993), 21.

[58] Peter Braun, *Form vollendet: Meissener Manuskripte XVIII* (Meissen: Staatliche Porzellan-Manufaktur Meissen, 2006).

[59] Otto Walcha, *Meissner Porzellan – Von den Anfängen bis zur Gegenwart* (Dresden: Verlag der Kunst, 1973), 128.

[60] Günter Reinheckel, "Plastische Dekorationsformen im Meisner Porzellan des 18. Jahrhunderts," *Keramos* 41-42 (1968): 78.

[61] Ibid., 78.

[62] Johan Willsberger and Rainer Rückert, *Meissen. Porzellan des 18. Jahrhunderts* (Regensburg: Walhalla und Praetoria, 2002), 43.

[63] Joachim Menzhausen, "Werdegang und Stil des Bildhauers Kändler," *Keramos* 175-176 (2002): 3-13.

[64] Johan Willsberger and Rainer Rückert, 49.

[65] Samuel Wittwer, *The Gallery of Meissen Animals: Augustus the Strong's Menagerie for the Japanese Palace in Dresden* (Munich: Hirmer, 2006), 93.

[66] Ibid., 93.

[67] Ulrich Pietsch, "Kaendler und Kirchner - Ein Stilvergleich," *Keramos* 198 (2007): 11.

[68] Ingelore Menzhausen and Jürgen Karpinski, *In Porzellan verzaubert* (Basel: Wiese, 1993), 20.

[69] Morley-Fletcher, Hugo. *Meissen Porcelain in Colour* (Exeter: Exeter Books, 1979), 32.

[70] Ulrich Pietsch, "Kaendler und Kirchner - Ein Stilvergleich," *Keramos* 198 (2007): 14.

[71] Otto Walcha, 94-95.

[72] Ingelore Menzhausen, *Early Meissen Porcelain in Dresden* (New York: Thames & Hudson Ltd, 1990), 8.

[73] Ingelore Menzhausen, "Horoldt und sein 'Seminarium' - Meisen, 1720 bis 1730," *Keramos* 120 (1988): 37.

[74] Peter Braun, "Bemerkungen zur Praxis der Meissener Modellwerkstatt unter Johann Joachim Kaendler," *Keramos* 194 (2006): 47.

[75] Karl Berling, *Königlich Sächsische Porzellanmanufactur Meissen: 1710 – 1910* (Leipzig: F A Brockhaus, 1911), 31.

[76] Ibid., 31.

[77] Kändler, 1739, quoted in Ingelore Menzhausen and Jürgen Karpinski, *In Porzellan verzaubert* (Basel: Wiese, 1993), 67.

[78] Maureen Cassidy-Geiger, "Meissen et la France avant et après la Guerre de Sept ans: Artistes, Espionnage et Commerce," in *XXes Rencontres de l'Ecole du Louvre: Art français et art allemand au XVIIIe siècle – regards croisés* (Paris, 2008), 69.

[79] Otto Walcha, 132.

[80] Maureen Cassidy-Geiger, 71.

[81] Otto Walcha, "Kaendlers Reiterdenkmal," *Keramos* 9 (1960): 11.

[82] Karl Berling, 40.

[83] Otto Walcha, "Kaendlers Reiterdenkmal," *Keramos* 9 (1960): 18-19.

[84] Karl Berling, 44.

[85] Ibid, 47.

[86] Günter Reinheckel, "Plastische Dekorationsformen im Meisner Porzellan des 18. Jahrhunderts," *Keramos* 41-42 (1968): 82.

[87] Ulrich Pietsch, *Schwanenservice: Meissener Porzellan für Heinrich Graf von Brühl* (Berlin: Edition Leipzig, 2000), 25.

[88] Günter Reinheckel, "Plastische Dekorationsformen im Meisner Porzellan des 18. Jahrhunderts," *Keramos* 41-42 (1968): 76.

[89] Hans Sonntag; " 'Alter' und 'Neuer' Ausschnitt -ein kurioses und feh-

lerhaftes Durcheinander in der Meissener Fachliteratur," *Keramos* 205 (2009): 8.

[90] Ulrich Pietsch, *Schwanenservice: Meissener Porzellan für Heinrich Graf von Brühl* (Berlin: Edition Leipzig, 2000), 25.

[91] Johan Willsberger and Rainer Rückert, 58.

[92] Günter Reinheckel, "Plastische Dekorationsformen im Meisner Porzellan des 18. Jahrhunderts," *Keramos* 41-42 (1968): 76.

[93] Ibid, 38.

[94] Ibid, 38.

[95] Uwe Beyer, *Einen Pfau in Lebens Groesse Modelliret...: Meissener Manuskripte XIX* (Meissen: Staatliche Porzellan-Manufaktur Meissen, 2006), 39.

[96] Ulrich Pietsch, *Schwanenservice: Meissener Porzellan für Heinrich Graf von Brühl* (Berlin: Edition Leipzig, 2000), 30.

[97] Nina Simone Schepkowski, "'Gotzkowsky erhabene Blumen': Ein Meissener Porzellanservice für Friedrich den Großen," *Keramos* 201 (2008): 28.

[98] Ibid, 30.

[99] Ingelore Menzhausen, "Horoldt und sein 'Seminarium' - Meisen, 1720 bis 1730," *Keramos* 120 (1988): 27.

[100] Ulrich Pietsch, *Schwanenservice: Meissener Porzellan für Heinrich Graf von Brühl* (Berlin: Edition Leipzig, 2000), 24.

[101] Joachim Kunze, "Zur Dekorationsbranche der Meißener Porzellanmanufaktur nach 1814 bis
zum Jahre 1860," *Keramos* 135 (1992): 24.

[102] Alexandra W. Troschinskaja, "Das außergewöhnliche Schicksal des Hofservices 'Roter Drache' von August dem Starken," *Keramos* 202 (2008): 71.

[103] Ibid, 67-68.

[104] Ibid, 68.

[105] Hans Sonntag and Jürgen Karpinski, *Die Sprache der Blumen. Meissener Porzellan* (Leipzig: Seemann, 1995), 15.

[106] Johan Willsberger and Rainer Rückert, 61.

[107] Karl Berling, 51.

[108] Johan Willsberger and Rainer Rückert, 55.

[109] Ulrich Pietsch, *Schwanenservice: Meissener Porzellan für Heinrich Graf von Brühl* (Berlin: Edition Leipzig, 2000), 25.

[110] Maureen Cassidy-Geiger, 71.

[111] Ulrich Pietsch (ed.), *Meissen for the Czars: Porcelain as a Means of Saxon-Russian Politics in the Eighteenth Century* (München: Hirmer, 2004), 66-85.

[112] Natalia Kasakiewitsch, "Entstehung und Geschichte des Andreas-Services," *Keramos* 149 (1995): 47.

[113] Ibid., 51.

[114] Ulrich Pietsch (ed.), *Meissen for the Czars: Porcelain as a Means of Saxon-Russian Politics in the Eighteenth Century* (München: Hirmer, 2004), 50-56.

[115] Ibid., 58-65.

[116] A large collection is shown and described in Pietsch, Ulrich, *Die figürliche Meissner Porzellanplastik von Gottlieb Kirchner und Johann Joachim Kaendler: Bestandskatalog der Porzellansammlung Staatliche Kunstsammlungen Dresden* (München: Hirmer, 2006), 90-121.

[117] See, for example, Charles Creighton, *The Fabulous Meissen Apostles* (Place of publication and publisher not identified, 1978).

[118] Ulrich Pietsch and Claudia Banz (eds.) *Triumph of the Blue Swords: Meissen Porcelain for Aristocracy and Bourgeoisie, 1710–1815* (Leipzig: Seemann E.a., 2010), 78.

[119] T. H. Clarke, "Die 'Römische Bestellung' - Die Meißener Altar-Garnitur, die August III. dem Kardinal Annibale Albani im Jahre 1736 schenkte," *Keramos* 86 (1979): 10.

[120] Ibid., 17-47.

[121] Ralph H. Wark, "Die Meißner Apostelfiguren von Johann J. Kaendler," *Keramos* 10 (1960): 176-177.

[122] Erich Köllmann, "Der Mopsorden," *Keramos* 50 (1970): 71.

[123] Daniela Antonin, "Historic Collectors: Clemens August," in Gerhard Röbbig, *Cabinet Pieces: The Meissen Porcelain Birds of Johann Joachim Kändler* (Munich: Hirmer Verlag Gmbh, 2008), 41.

[124] Erich Köllmann, 72.

[125] Hans Sonntag and Jürgen Karpinski, *Erlebte Kunst: Meissener Figurenporzellan aus drei Jahrhunderten* (Leipzig: Edition Leipzig, 1997), 11-12.

[126] Ulrich Pietsch, *Die figürliche Meissner Porzellanplastik von Gottlieb*

Kirchner und Johann Joachim Kaendler (München: Hirmer, 2006), 34-49.

[127] Günter Reinheckel, "Die erste Folge der Pariser Ausrufer in Meißner Porzellan," *Keramos* 50 (1970): 117.

[128] Ibid., 117-119.

[129] Ibid., 115.

[130] Ulrich Pietsch and Claudia Banz (eds.) *Triumph of the Blue Swords: Meissen Porcelain for Aristocracy and Bourgeoisie, 1710–1815* (Leipzig: Seemann E.a., 2010), 72.

[131] Gerhard Lehmann, "Betrachtungen zur Folge der Bergmannsfiguren von J. J. Kaendler," *Keramos* 167-168 (2000): 203.

[132] Ibid., 204.

[133] Ibid.

[134] Ibid., 212.

[135] Christoph Fritzsche, "Eine Affenkapelle der Porzellanmanufaktur Pößek - ihr Meissener Vorbild und Affenkapellen weiterer Manufakturen," *Keramos* 225 (2014): 113-132.

[136] Yvonne Hackenbroth and Ernst Zimmerman cited in Christoph Fritzsche, "Eine Affenkapelle der Porzellanmanufaktur Pößek - ihr Meissener Vorbild und Affenkapellen weiterer Manufakturen," *Keramos* 225 (2014): 116-118.

[137] Hans Sonntag, *Die Affenkapelle aus Meissener Porzellan* (Frankfurt am Main: Insel, 1993), 40.

[138] Hans Sonntag and Jürgen Karpinski, *Erlebte Kunst: Meissener Figurenporzellan aus drei Jahrhunderten* (Leipzig: Edition Leipzig, 1997), 46.

[139] Hans Sonntag, "Auf der Spurensuche nach den malerischen und grafischen Vorlagen für die Meissener 'Affenkapelle' von Johann Joachim Kaendler und Peter Reinicke," *Keramos* 193 (2006): 12.

[140] Ibid, 3 & 8-9.

[141] Ibid, 14.

[142] Uwe Beyer, *Einen Pfau in Lebens Groesse Modelliret...: Meissener Manuskripte XIX* (Meissen: Staatliche Porzellan-Manufaktur Meissen, 2006), 53.

[143] Ingelore Menzhausen and Jürgen Karpinski, *In Porzellan verzaubert* (Basel: Wiese, 1993), 28.

[144] Otto Walcha, "Fröhlich und Schmiedel im Meißner Porzellan," *Keramos* 32 (1966): 35.

[145] Günter Reinheckel, "Plastische Dekorationsformen im Meisner Porzellan des 18. Jahrhunderts," *Keramos* 41-42 (1968): 85.

[146] Ibid, 92.

[147] For an overview of his orders, see Britzke, Brigitte. *Friedrich der Große und seine Porzellanbestellungen in Meißen während des Siebenjährigen Krieges*. Bad Pyrmont: Museumsverein im Schloss Pyrmont e.V., 2012.

[148] Günter Reinheckel, "Plastische Dekorationsformen im Meisner Porzellan des 18. Jahrhunderts," *Keramos* 41-42 (1968): 90.

[149] Rainer Rückert, "Wiener und Meisener Porzellangeschirr des 18. Jahrhunderts 'Alla Turca,'" *Keramos* 147 (1995): 52-63.

[150] Ibid, 5.

[151] Ibid, 63.

[152] Maureen Cassidy-Geiger, 73.

[153] Ibid, 74.

[154] Karl Berling, 69.

[155] Otto Walcha, *Meissner Porzellan – Von den Anfängen bis zur Gegenwart* (Dresden: Verlag der Kunst, 1973), 156.

[156] Karl Berling, *Königlich Sächsische Porzellanmanufactur Meissen: 1710 – 1910* (Leipzig: F A Brockhaus, 1911), 70.

[157] Ulrich Pietsch and Claudia Banz (eds.) *Triumph of the Blue Swords: Meissen Porcelain for Aristocracy and Bourgeoisie, 1710–1815* (Leipzig: Seemann E.a., 2010), 391.

[158] Pauline Gräfin von Spee, *Die klassizistische Porzellanplastik der Meissener Manufaktur von 1764 bis 1814* (Unpublished doctoral dissertation, Rheinische Friedrich-Wilhelms-Universität Bonn, 2004), 86.

[159] Ulrich Pietsch and Claudia Banz, 392.

[160] Hans Sonntag, "Jean Troy aus Lunéville - auf Spurensuche nach dem fast vergessenen Modelleur aus Lothringen," *Keramos* 209 (2010): 39.

[161] An overview and description can be found in Hans Sonntag, "Jean Troy aus Lunéville - auf Spurensuche nach dem fast vergessenen Modelleur aus Lothringen," *Keramos* 209 (2010): 42-49.

[162] Hans Sonntag, " 'Inès' und 'Mimi', die Lieblingshunde der Marquise de Pompadur – 2008 aus Meissener Porzellan zu neuem Leben erweckt," *Keramos* 200 (2008): 30.

[163] Pauline Gräfin von Spee, 112.

[164] Ulrich Pietsch (ed.), *Meissen for the czars: porcelain as a means of*

Saxon-Russian politics in the eighteenth century (München: Hirmer, 2004), 7.

[165] Ibid, 95.

[166] A detailed description of each of the 40 figurines can be found in Pauline Gräfin von Spee, 222-233 and 288-307.

[167] Erich Köllmann, "Die Porzellanservice des Herzogs von Wellington," *Keramos* 10 (1960): 81.

[168] Ulrich Pietsch (ed.), *Meissen for the czars: porcelain as a means of Saxon-Russian politics in the eighteenth century* (München: Hirmer, 2004), 38.

[169] Joachim Kunze, "Die Porzellanmanufaktur Meißen am Ende ihrer Marcoliniperiode in den Jahren 1810 bis 1813," *Keramos* 111 (1986): 5.

[170] Otto Walcha, *Meissner Porzellan – Von den Anfängen bis zur Gegenwart* (Dresden: Verlag der Kunst, 1973), 178.

[171] Otto Walcha, "Die Marcolini-Zeit der Meißner Manufaktur," *Keramos* 40 (1968): 36.

[172] Ibid, 32.

[173] Pauline Gräfin von Spee, 92.

[174] Otto Walcha, "Die Marcolini-Zeit der Meißner Manufaktur," *Keramos* 40 (1968): 32.

[175] Willi Goder, "Johann Carl Schönheit zwischen Kaendler und Acier," *Keramos* 114 (1986): 25.

[176] Otto Walcha, "Die Marcolini-Zeit der Meißner Manufaktur," *Keramos* 40 (1968): 34.

[177] Pauline Gräfin von Spee, 133-134.

[178] Ibid, 140.

[179] See Peter-Christian Wegner, "Literatur auf Porzellan - Ovids 'Metamorphosen' auf Meißner Porzellan der Marcolini-Zeit," *Keramos* 207 (2010): 61-68.

[180] See Peter-Christian Wegner, "Literatur auf Porzellan - Abälard und Heloise. Die 'Leidensgeschichte' und die 'Briefe' in Popescher Manier auf Meißner Porzellan der Marcolini-Zeit," *Keramos* 202 (2008): 39-50.

[181] See Peter-Christian Wegner, "Literatur auf Porzellan - Langhornes 'Theodosius and Constantia' auf einer Meißner Tasse der Marcolini-Zeit," *Keramos* 202 (2008): 51-56.

[182] Joachim Kunze, "Vergoldungsarten für Porzellane der Meißner

Manufaktur in der ersten Hälfte des 19. Jahrhunderts," *Keramos* 99 (1983): 43.

[183] Joachim Kunze, "Beitrag zur Geschichte der Porzellanmanufaktur Meißen in der Biedermeierzeit," *Keramos* 86 (1979): 60.

[184] Johannes Just, *Meissen porcelain and the art nouveau period* (Cincinnati: Seven Hills Books, 1985), 8.

[185] Joachim Kunze, "Vergoldungsarten für Porzellane der Meißner Manufaktur in der ersten Hälfte des 19. Jahrhunderts," *Keramos* 99 (1983): 44.

[186] Ibid, 45.

[187] Ibid.

[188] Ibid.

[189] Joachim Kunze, "Zur Dekorationsbranche der Meißener Porzellanmanufaktur nach 1814 bis
zum Jahre 1860," *Keramos* 135 (1992): 7.

[190] Antje Borrmann, Birgit Finger, and Simona Schellenberger (eds), *Kunst oder Kommerz?: Meissener Porzellan im 19. Jahrhundert* (Dresden: Staatliche Schlösse, Burgen und Gärten Sachsen: Sandstein, 2010), 121.

[191] Joachim Kunze, "Einführung und Verwendung der Chromoxidgrunfarbe bei der Porzellanmanufaktur Meißen ab 1817," *Keramos* 106 (1984): 19.

[192] Antje Borrmann, Birgit Finger, and Simona Schellenberger, 120.

[193] Joachim Kunze, 22.

[194] Pauline Gräfin von Spee, 167.

[195] Joachim Kunze, "Porzellanpfeifen der Meißener Manufaktur nach 1814," *Keramos* 116 (1987): 15.

[196] Joachim Kunze, "Lithophanien der Meißner Porzellanmanufaktur," *Keramos* 92 (1981): 3.

[197] Ibid, 4.

[198] Rüdiger van Dick, "Lithophanien der Meißner Porzellanmanufaktur. Eine Ergänzung zum gleichlautenden Beitrag von Joachim Kunze," *Keramos* 109 (1985): 18.

[199] Antje Borrmann, Birgit Finger, and Simona Schellenberger, 118.

[200] Ibid.

[201] Rüdiger van Dick, 21.

[202] Joachim Kunze, "Lithophanien der Meißner Porzellanmanufaktur," *Keramos* 92 (1981): 6.

[203] Antje Borrmann, Birgit Finger, and Simona Schellenberger, 34.

[204] Erich Köllmann, "Die Porzellanservice des Herzogs von Wellington," *Keramos* 10 (1960): 86-88.

[205] Joachim Kunze, "Ein Beitrag zu den Formen Meißner Porzellangeschirre von 1814 bis nach 1830," *Keramos* 102 (1983): 3.

[206] Antje Borrmann, Birgit Finger, and Simona Schellenberger, 28.

[207] Joachim Kunze, "Porzellanerden für die Manufaktur Meißen nach 1814," *Keramos* 126 (1989): 31.

[208] Joachim Kunze, "Einführung und Verwendung der Chromoxidgrunfarbe bei der Porzellanmanufaktur Meißen ab 1817," *Keramos* 106 (1984): 22.

[209] Antje Borrmann, Birgit Finger, and Simona Schellenberger, 79.

[210] Joachim Kunze, "Einführung und Verwendung der Chromoxidgrunfarbe bei der Porzellanmanufaktur Meißen ab 1817," *Keramos* 106 (1984): 25.

[211] Ibid, 24.

[212] Antje Borrmann, Birgit Finger, and Simona Schellenberger, 26.

[213] Joachim Kunze, "Zur Dekorationsbranche der Meißener Porzellanmanufaktur nach 1814 bis zum Jahre 1860," *Keramos* 135 (1992): 23.

[214] Joachim Kunze, "Meißner Porzellane nach Glaskristallmustern (1831 bis 1855)," *Keramos* 105 (1984): 17-34.

[215] Joachim Kunze, "Von der Albrechtsburg in das Triebischtal - Hintergründe der Produktionsverlegung der Meißner Porzellanmanufaktur nach 1850," *Keramos* 109 (1985): 35.

[216] Ibid, 37.

[217] Ibid, 40.

[218] Antje Borrmann, Birgit Finger, and Simona Schellenberger, 91-92.

[219] Ibid, 124.

[220] Johannes Just, *Meissen porcelain and the art nouveau period* (Cincinnati: Seven Hills Books, 1985), 13.

[221] Ibid, 14.

[222] Hermann Jedding, *Meißener Porzellan des 19. und 20. Jahrhunderts 1800 - 1933.* (München: Keysersche Verlagsbuchhandlung, 1993), 11.

[223] Antje Borrmann, Birgit Finger, and Simona Schellenberger, 103-105.

[224] Johannes Just, *Meissen Porcelain and the Art Nouveau Period* (Cincinnati: Seven Hills Books, 1985), 7.

[225] An overview of his works can be found in Hans Sonntag, "Karl Theodor Eichler (1868-1946) - ein Meissener Porzellanplastiker des frühen 20. Jahrhunderts," *Keramos* 224 (2014): 37-38.

[226] Marush-Krohn, Caren. *Meissener Porzellan 1918–1933: Die Pfeifferzeit* (Leipzig: Edition Leipzig, 1993), 21.

[227] Ibid, 20.

[228] Christian Lechelt, "Emil Paul Börner (1888-1970) - Ein Künstler, der Probleme macht ...," *Keramos* 211-212 (2011): 115.

[229] Helmut Dämmig, *Meißner Porzellanglockenspiele*, (Meissen: Thieme, 1987), 6-8.

[230] Ibid, 33-70.

[231] Reineking von Bock, Gisela, "Paul Scheurich", Mitteilungsblatt Nr. 100, Keramik-Freunde der Schweiz, (Zurich, 1985), 16.

[232] Christian Lechelt, 116.

[233] Erich Schrauber, "Die Entwicklung der Porzellanmanufaktur von 1945 bis zur Gegenwart," in *250 Jahre Staatliche Porzellan-Manufaktur Meissen.* (Meissen: publisher, 1960), 91.

[234] Ibid, 94.

[235] Ibid, 98.

[236] Otto Walcha, *Meissner Porzellan – Von den Anfängen bis zur Gegenwart* (Dresden: Verlag der Kunst, 1973), 206.

[237] Robert E. Röntgen, *The Book of Meissen* (Exton, PA: Schiffer Pub Ltd, 1996), 10.

[238] Ibid.

[239] Ulrich Pietsch and Peter Ufer, *Mythos Meissen: das erste Porzellan Europas* (Dresden: Ed. Sächs. Zeitung, 2008), 53

[240] Robert E. Röntgen, 11.

[241] Ibid, 44.

[242] Ulrich Pietsch and Peter Ufer, 88.

[243] Ibid, 78.

[244] Ibid, 79.

[245] Hans Sonntag, "Frauen bei Meissen," *Keramos* 211-212 (2011): 136.

[246] Günter Reinheckel, "... Eine Sache so noch nie in der Welt gemachet ... Orgelpfeifen aus Meissener Porzellan," *Keramos* 173 (2001): 48.

[247] Ibid, 49.

[248] Ibid.

[249] Hans Sonntag, "Frauen bei Meissen," *Keramos* 211-212 (2011): 128.

[250] Ibid, 132.

[251] Ibid, 134.

[252] Ibid, 137.

[253] Ibid, 140.

[254] Ibid, 143.

[255] Ibid, 35-47.

[256] Ingelore Menzhausen and Jürgen Karpinski, *In Porzellan verzaubert* (Basel: Wiese, 1993), 66.

[257] Julia Weber, The Height of Luxury: Ormolu mounts and porcelain flowers, in Gerhard Röbbig, *Cabinet Pieces: The Meissen Porcelain Birds of Johann Joachim Kändler* (Munich: Hirmer Verlag Gmbh, 2008), 64.

[258] Ulrich Pietsch, *Zauber der Zerbrechlichkeit: Meisterwerke europäischer Porzellankunst* (Leipzig: Seemann, 2010), 18.